TABLE OF CONTENTS

Page

CHAPTER

LIST OF ILLUSTRATIONS

CHAPTER 1

INTRODUCTION

It is best to win without fighting and fight once rather than twice. The strategist must pick his time and place, strike when the situation is in his favor, and prevail quickly.[1]

Sun Tzu

This thesis begins to address one of the most pressing and interesting national security issues confronting the United States in the post-cold war era and into the twenty-first century: China. Much has been addressed in the press, academia, and certainly in the policy-making organs of states throughout the world with regard to the dissolution of the Soviet Union and the geopolitical and strategic implications for the rest of the world. The United States remains the world's only superpower and will likely remain so for the next twenty-five years according to most experts.[2] However, one cannot address the issue of the post-cold war era without looking over the Western horizon. Some look over this horizon with anxiety and a sense of foreboding. Others anticipate the arrival of a new era of economic opportunity and prosperity, confident that increasing economic interdependence among the nations of the world will foster stability and cooperation. Most agree that the future developments among nations will depend to a large degree upon the future developments of China. China's current economic growth, military modernization, population, national ambitions, and engagement in world affairs will

---

[1]Sun Tzu, *The Art of War*, trans. with a forward by Samuel B. Griffith (Oxford, London: Oxford University Press, 1971), 79.

[2]Bates Gill and Lonnie Henley, *China and the RMA* (Carlisle Barracks, PA: Strategic Studies Institute, US Army War College, 1996), 55.

1

place it at the center of international affairs in the next century. The critical question is, Will China's development and future relationships with Asia and the international community be characterized by confrontation or cooperation?[3]

There is a great scholarly and policy debate over China's intentions toward her neighbors. All agree that China is modernizing its economy, industry, and its military capabilities. Richard Bernstein and Ross Munro, a journalist and a scholar, contend this drive is a function of China's aspirations to become a regional hegemonic power, driven by a desire to overcome a century of impotence and humiliation, to restore its rightful place as the "Middle Kingdom." They argue nationalism has replaced communist ideology and represents no less a threat. Yet other scholars, like Andrew J. Nathan and Robert S. Ross, contend that this is part of securing legitimate national interest, pursuing economic development, and peaceful and mutually beneficial relations with her neighbors and the world. Which view is correct and how can one make this determination?

There are many approaches. Scholars, such as Richard J. Smith, have studied Chinese history to identify recurring historical patterns and ancient Chinese military stratagems, many of which are still relevant today. Others look at the role of influential individuals, while still others take a realist perspective, focusing on geopolitical factors which have changed little over time. Often, similar approaches offer different conclusions, while providing important insights to the general question. Yet much uncertainty remains, as it must when addressing the future.

---

[3]Daniel Bergen, *Fueling Asia's Recovery* (NY: Council on Foreign Relations, Inc., Foreign Affairs, March-April 1998).

This inquiry will analyze the veracity of Chinese (People's Republic of China) statements of its interests and intentions vis-a-vis its regional neighbors and the international community. It is inspired by the Chinese White Paper on National Defense released on 30 July 1998. This document is a useful and relevant starting point. It is replete with benign assertions of Chinese interests in promoting mutual cooperation, trust, development, and security through the peaceful resolution of differences. Taken at face value the future certainly looks bright. However, in the conduct of international affairs, actions speak louder than words and history sits in judgment. The critical question of China's intentions remains, particularly in light of Sun Zi, the great Chinese strategist, who observed that "War is a game of deception. Therefore, feign incapability when in fact capable; feign inactivity when ready to strike; appear to be far away when actually nearby, and vice versa."[4] Can China be trusted?

This analysis begins by examining the Chinese white paper on national defense in greater detail. The document was provided to the world by the Chinese Information Office of the State Council.[5] Its central element is the reiteration of the five principles of peaceful coexistence, originally announced at the 1954 Bandung Conference. These principles are: (1) mutual respect for territorial integrity and sovereignty, (2) mutual nonaggression, (3) noninterference in each other's internal affairs, (4) equality and mutual benefit, and (5) peaceful coexistence. All countries should strengthen mutually beneficial

---

[4]M. V. Rappai, *China's Military Modernization: Some Perspectives* (IDSA, 1998); available from http://www.idsa-india.org/an-jan-2.html; Internet; accessed 28 August 1998.

[5]Periscope Special Reports, *China White Paper on New Concept of International Security*; available from http://www.periscope.ucg.com/nations/asia/china; Internet; accessed 28 August 1998.

cooperation and eliminate inequalities and discriminatory policies in economic and trade relations, gradually reducing the economic gap between countries. Strengthening regional and international economic contacts and cooperation would create a stable and secure external economic environment, becoming the economic basis for regional and global security. Furthermore, the white paper emphasizes that each country has a right to choose its own social system, development strategy, and way of life; and no country should interfere in the internal affairs of any other country in any way or under any pretext, much less resort to military threats or aggression. Mutual understanding and trust through dialogue and cooperation would promote the peaceful settlement of disputes among nations.[6]

The white paper asserts that Chinese defense policy is defensive; that disputes should be solved by nonmilitary means; and that strategic mastery would be gained by striking only after the enemy has struck. It further elaborates on consolidating the national defense, resisting aggression, curbing armed subversion, and defending the state's sovereignty, unity, territorial integrity, and security by military means. The stated rationale is that as long as hegemonism and power politics still exist, a country must have the capability to defend its legitimate interests. To exercise this right, China is modernizing its armed forces, but only to secure its legitimate defensive needs. The white paper further states that the development of the national defense is subordinate to and in the service of China's overall economic construction. However, at the same time,

---

[6]Foreign Broadcast Information Service (FBIS), *Chinese White Paper on National Defense* (Beijing, Xinhua: Information Office of the State Council of China, 27 July 1998).

in view of the characteristics of modern wars, no effort would be spared to improve the modernization level of weaponry, reform and perfect the army system, and setup and improve the training of troops, curricula, and teaching methods of the military academies. The goal is to improve quality and streamline the army in a Chinese way, aiming to form a revolutionized, modernized, and regularized people's army with Chinese characteristics.

What are current and future Chinese aspirations? Chapter 2 will examine this question in greater detail. The recurring and generally agreed upon themes are: (1) expanding trade to generate capital to finance modernization and continued development; (2) acquiring science and technology to modernize economically and militarily; (3) assuring regional stability to facilitate trade; (4) territorial defense; (5) unification with Taiwan; and (6) securing territorial claims in dispute with other nations. The latter two objectives create the greatest anxiety for the international community and cause many to challenge Chinese platitudes of peaceful cooperation as well as the defensive posture outlined in the white paper. To China, Taiwan is a domestic issue, as is unrest in Inner Mongolia, Tibet, and Xinjiang and is therefore outside the purview of international affairs. Consequently, one encounters the recurring Chinese refrain of respect for territorial integrity, sovereignty, and noninterference in upholding the five principles of peaceful coexistence. The Spratly and Paracel Islands disputes are yet another example of Chinese implacability on issues pertaining to sovereignty and territorial integrity (though some concessions have been made with respect to the Spratlys). It is instructive to note that China has employed military force in these disputes as well as in disputes with India, Russia, and Vietnam since 1954. These domestic issues are not likely to be

5

discussed, particularly in light of the results of political liberalization in the Soviet Union, the dissolution of the Soviet state, and accompanying ethnic violence. China's leaders clearly understand that given the Chinese state's transnational character, it cannot survive if any one of the provinces attains greater autonomy. This factor, as well as its experience at Tiananmen Square, serves to highlight the regime's domestic vulnerability.

Yet clearly, the use of the military to achieve China's national ambitions, given China's current challenges, enormous potential, and dependency on international trade and technologies, would seem to fail any rational cost benefit analysis. This is easily evident in the short term, while China is building the economy, industrial and technical infrastructure, and relatively backward military. But what of the long term, where China will likely wield tremendous economic influence and have invested billions of dollars into transforming the People's Liberation Army from a territorial defense force to a force capable of projecting power beyond China's immediate borders? China's historical perspective has always been long term relative to the West. This is reinforced in this century by Mao's concept of protracted war. Time is relative to nations and not nearly as important a concept as national will and perseverance is to the Chinese. Given the seemingly inevitability of China's ascendance economically and militarily, will China couple her economic capability with military ambitions? Bernstein and Munro fear an economically strong and militarily capable China and assert that once China modernizes her economy and military, it is only a matter of time before both will be employed to support aggressive and expansionist designs. They view China's current rapprochement and openness as a tactical gesture rather than a strategic shift to a more interdependent and integrated world.[7]

The importance of China's role in the future cannot be overstated. China is the most populous nation in the world, with virtually inexhaustible human capital. It is a nuclear power with the world's third largest nuclear arsenal and with the largest conventional army. It is a permanent member of the United Nations Security Council. China is actively engaged in world affairs and wields considerable influence over third world members in the United Nations General Assembly. Not only is China undergoing rapid economic and military modernization, Chinese society is experiencing the profound changes associated with the transition from a command economy to a "socialist market economy," as well as undergoing the incumbent expectations of an improved life for the average Chinese citizen, with considerable implications for political stability. China's governing elite, though still communist, no longer commands the demigod status as once had the revolutionary old guard of Mao Zedung, Zhou Enlai, or even Deng Xiaoping. In international affairs, only the United States and China are capable of exerting any real influence on North Korea. China's ability and demonstrated willingness to export nuclear and missile technologies has a direct impact on regional security balances in western Asia and the Middle East. Finally, as a growing economic power and developing country, China will both compete for limited resources and exert tremendous pressures on trade balances with developed and developing nations. Furthermore, the modernization of

[7]Richard Bernstein and Ross Munro, *The Coming Conflict with China* (New York: Alfred A. Knopf, Inc., 1997).

Chinese industry and the expansion of its economy will have significant environmental impacts on China's neighbors.

These are only the most salient issues which make China central to regional security considerations in the twenty-first century. A clear understanding of China's experiences, perspectives, legitimate security needs, national interests, and ambitions is necessary to effectively engage China on the above issues. The world cannot risk engaging China with wishful thinking. Neither can the world reflexively resist China's legitimate needs and err by creating a self-fulfilling prophecy. The question then arises: What constitutes legitimate security needs?

The relevance and importance of the subject being outlined, it is necessary to once again go back to the original dilemma. Can China be trusted to act in accord with the goals articulated at Bandung and in the 1998 white paper? What means can the US use to make this determination? The US is already challenged in making the assumption that it, culturally distinct from China (one of the most nuanced cultures in the world) is capable of correctly perceiving China's internal and external requirements and dilemmas through the prism of a Western superpower with a completely alien and, in Asian terms, relatively brief history. One must of necessity examine China's history as well as her present to understand the context of her decisions. Though necessary, this subjects the analyst and scholar to the fallacy of reasoning by "false analogies" as they apply their own history and biased perspectives to the Chinese, unless great care is made in looking at the specific circumstances of events and, most importantly, the perceptions and perspectives of the

Chinese at that given time.[8] The improper use of history may also cause one to conduct the "opposite wrong," as one takes solutions to the mistakes of the past and blindly applies them to problems of the present or the future.[9]

With this in mind, the author will in this thesis compare and contrast Chinese statements with Chinese actions in three crises since 1949. What did China say, what did China do, and what was the context? Also, the author will identify consistent patterns of Chinese national and strategic thought regarding national interests, foreign relations, conflict, and ways this is translated into policy and transmitted to potential adversaries. Understanding these possible patterns will provide a way to assess Chinese intentions and possible motivations in future regional crisis and thereby help decision makers understand the consequences of their decisions.

The specific historical case studies the author will examine in chapters 3, 4, and 5, are: (1) China's 1950 intervention in Korea; (2) the 1962 border war with India; and (3) the 1979 invasion of Vietnam. Time and space precludes dealing with the period before 1949. No attempt will be made to analyze China's border conflict with the Soviet Union on the Amur River in 1960 and 1969. Since China views questions involving Taiwan, Tibet, Xinjiang, and the South China Sea as questions involving sovereignty, nationalism, and territorial integrity, reference will not be made to them, except when relevant to the primary discussion. This study defines "China" as the People's Republic of China defines China, including the territories of Tibet and Taiwan. It will use the prevailing form of

---

[8]John G. Stoessinger, *Why Nations Go to War* (Boston: Goughton Mifflin Co., 1983).

[9]Richard Neustadt and Ernest May, *Thinking in Time* (New York: Free Press, 1988).

9

Chinese spelling and pronunciation for the period addressed, changing name romanization styles depending on the era examined and the most commonly recognized form of the name.

The author is a realist in diplomatic matters. The author assumes that China's strategic interests in security and foreign affairs are no different than that of any other nation. He also assumes Chinese leaders rationally apply a cost benefit analysis in determining their strategic and geopolitical interests and in determining the best policy to pursue those interests. In each case, the author will answer the following questions to determine recurring patterns in Chinese approaches to conflict:

1. What were the events leading up to the crisis?

2. What was its overall strategic context?

3. What was the perspective of the Chinese leadership?

4. What were the prevailing perceptions and why?

5. What statements were made by China, and how were they made?

6. What were China's intentions and objectives in making the statements?

7. What were the unintended consequences?

8. What capabilities and alternatives were available to China?

9. What action was taken relative to statements made?

10. Did the Chinese make deliberately deceptive statements?

11. What was the outcome and how did it relate to Chinese goals?

The answers to these questions should help provide an understanding of how China perceives its role and the role of others in the conduct of regional affairs in Asia. This is outlined in chapter 6.

After reading the thesis, the reader should be able to determine whether or not Chinese policy contains any cultural, individual, or institutional tendencies to clearly address its interests to the international community regarding international affairs and conflict or whether there is a tendency to dissemble. What were the elements of policy consistently weighed by Chinese decision makers which were followed through beyond diplomatic brinkmanship to the battlefield? How were these policy interests signaled to its adversaries? Most important, what can be learned from these conflicts and incorporated into future policy formulation to avoid conflict?

CHAPTER 2

LITERATURE REVIEW: OPPOSING POINTS OF VIEW

> No form of misunderstanding is more common in international
> affairs than the ascription of emotional or cultural irrationality to
> policies that are grounded in strategic motives.[1]

Andrew Nathan and Robert Ross

Given China's long history and significance in the world, there are innumerable

sources for the study of history, culture, and politics. This discussion focuses primarily

on differing perspectives in the most recent literature on Chinese political and strategic

thought. It will also examine the primary literature used to support each case study. Two

schools of thought dominate the literature: those who believe that China is not a threat if

properly engaged in the international community and those who believe that China is an

aggressive and expansionist state seeking regional hegemony and must therefore be

contained. There also exists a third school of thought which holds that China is too

politically unstable, too ethnically and culturally diverse, and too economically focused to

represent an external threat. According to this view, China will by necessity be focused

inward to maintain its diminishing political influence over its semi-autonomous provinces

and regions.

Andrew J. Nathan and Robert S. Ross coauthored *The Great Wall and the Empty

Fortress*. The central thesis to the work is that the rise of China need not present a threat

to international and regional stability if relations with China are properly managed.

---

[1]Andrew J. Nathan and Robert S. Ross, *The Great Wall and the Empty Fortress* (New York: W. W. Norton and Company, 1997).

Nathan and Ross assert that China is essentially a weak state with a foreign policy which is primarily defensive in nature. In contrast to other nations, Chinese decisions to use force were always made with the goal of defending home territory or deterring a perceived threat of invasion. Nathan and Ross also point out that historic mutual suspicions have subsided over time as a result of a converging regional security interest in limiting Soviet and Vietnamese expansion. They acknowledge that China (which shares borders with sixteen states) has unresolved territorial disputes with Russia, Tajikistan, North Korea, Vietnam, India, Japan, Malaysia, Philippines, and Brunei; however, they point out that China attempted to negotiate a settlement with each country concerned. Perhaps most significantly for the United States, Nathan and Ross assert that China possesses no vital interests beyond Asia.

According to the authors, China is at the same time both strong and weak. In this view, China is geopolitically weak and vulnerable, surrounded by numerous real and potential threats to its territory and to its sovereignty. Historically, China has been invaded by inner Asian neighbors five times and suffered incursions by Russia, Japan, and the European powers. China's culture is not predisposed to either war or peace and its policy is based upon legitimate security interests rather than a quest for hegemony. "Internally, Chinese society has been violent when weak government, economic disorder, or social dislocation made violence attractive, peaceful when it was well governed and prosperous. . . . Violence is a matter not of culture but of need and opportunity."[2] Furthermore, Nathan and Ross state that China's growing strength does not constitute a

---

[2]Ibid., 227.

13

threat to the region but rather a beneficial balance of power promoting stability and the status quo. They observe that China is regionally more secure now than at any time in the last 150 years[3] and has sought to resolve most international disputes by peaceful means. China's domestic challenges of population control, political unity, and economic modernization will prevent China from becoming an expansionist state. China's greatest threat is internal, based on the Soviet experience with liberalization and the 1989 Chinese prodemocracy demonstrations. Additionally, the authors assert that China is seeking to join the international community rather than to undermine it, as evidenced by its involvement in multiple international governmental and nongovernmental agencies and forums. Furthermore, China is consciously moving toward compliance with international regimes on trade, arms and technology transfers, and the environment.

Nathan and Ross assert that China seeks a balance of power within the region. China's current policy is driven by political realism and national interest, rather than ideology. Fear of a resurgent Japan and Russia plays a large role in policy formulation. Chinese policy is remarkably consistent with regard to the five principles declaration at Bandung and focuses on the maintenance of regional stability which is necessary to further develop beneficial trade ties. Without trade, China will be unable to develop the capital necessary to modernize its economy. Nevertheless, China has used military means to enforce its territorial claims. China's national interests lie primarily in the maintenance of trade, accession to the world trade organization, countering US and Russian collusion, denying any single power from becoming dominant in the region,

[3]Ibid., 21.

14

internal integrity and sovereignty of the state, continued US presence in the region to deter both North Korean adventures and Japanese rearmament. Specific goals include the denial of global recognition to Taiwan, gaining influence over smaller countries with regard to the formulation of international regimes and norms, and establishing itself as the natural leader of the non-West, nonwealthy nations of the world.[4]

Territorial integrity include the sensitive issues of Taiwan, Tibet, Inner Mongolia, Xinjiang, and the Spratly Islands. The authors contend that the Spratley Islands are too small to support airfields and power projection facilities, and that they in fact require a force projection capability that China does not have.[5] China has claimed the island chain since the Qing Dynasty. Any retreat undermines claims in other disputes and subjects China to the ramifications of such a compromise of territorial integrity and sovereignty.

According to Nathan and Ross, Chinese conflicts and aggressive behavior are borne of perceived threats to China's security, many of which are real. Chinese intervention in the Korean conflict was predicated on the very real fear of US forces continuing the conflict beyond liberating North Korea to liberating China on behalf of the Chinese Nationalists. China's conflict with India was a response to India's aspiration for regional dominance. India's capability to destabilize Chinese sovereignty over Tibet and Russian influence over India vis-a-vis China. China viewed India as facilitating the construction of a Soviet hostile arc around it aimed at isolating China from South Asia

---

[4]Ibid., 133-134.

[5]Ibid., 117.

15

and weakening China's ally Pakistan.[6] Chinese conflict with the Soviets, though initially

borne of Khrushchev's failure to consult Mao before attacking Stalin in a secret speech to

the 20th Party Congress in 1956, was attributed to Russia's high-handedness in the

relationship and ultimately the perception that China was being sacrificed to a Russian-

US rapprochement. Furthermore, the Soviet withdrawal of technical support to China's

nuclear weapons program and support of India heightened China's suspicions, as did

attempts to inhibit Chinese economic and industrial development during the Great Leap

Forward.[7] China's conflict with Vietnam was also couched in China's legitimate fear of

the expansion of Soviet influence in the region. China backed Pol Pot and the Khmer

Rouge rather than allow Soviet and Vietnamese domination of Indochina.

Nathan and Ross view China's policies with respect to Taiwan as being governed

by the same principles that govern the status of Xinjiang, Inner Mongolia, Tibet, and the

South China Sea Islands: to allow self-determination based on cultural distinctness would

establish a precedent for other territories seeking autonomy.[8] China's interest in the

region is the same as US interests in Cuba. Keep China's strategic backyard free of

foreign military influence.[9]

With respect to military modernization, Nathan and Ross point out that Chinese

strategic planners must plan against a revitalized Russia; a less-cooperative, unified, and

---

[6]Ibid., 119.

[7]Ibid., 42.

[8]Ibid., 206.

[9]Ibid., 64.

16

nuclear Korea; and a remilitarized Japan in the possession of sophisticated conventional

and strategic weaponry, power projection capabilities, and considerable economic

might.[10] The dilemma is that as China races to modernize, it risks stimulating its

neighbors to accelerate their own pace of advance, potentially widening rather than

narrowing the gap between Chinese security needs and military capabilities.[11]

With regard to Chinese defense expenditures and military modernization, the

authors point out that in real dollar terms, expenditures remained virtually steady into the

1990s and when corrected for inflation, were in the range of $6 billion per year, compared

to US defense budget of $270 billion and Japan defense budget of $42 billion per year.[12]

They point out that most specialists agree that official Chinese budget declarations are

understated by a factor of two to four times, as Chinese defense budget figures do not

incorporate military research and development, acquisitions, and ambiguous profits made

by military business enterprises.[13] Nevertheless, even when factoring in these figures,

they believe that the amount remains considerably less than Japan's expenditures in

absolute terms. "Adjusted for inflation and assessed as a share of the national budget,

China's defense expenditures may have even declined from early 1980 to the mid-

1990s."[14]

---

[10]Ibid., 144.

[11]Ibid., 138.

[12]Ibid., 147.

[13]Ibid., 147.

[14]Ibid., 148.

Despite purchases of Soviet and Israeli equipment (SU-24 ground attack aircraft, Kilo class submarines, SA-10 surface-to-air missiles, and airborne radar systems), the Chinese army possesses no real power-projection capabilities, and the PLA (including the air force and navy) remains primarily a defensive force. Nathan and Ross assert that China will not have the capability to produce an aircraft carrier and supporting fleet until 2010 at the earliest, and even if able to do so, there exists no guarantee that its attempt to do so will not result in a regional arms race which would only leave China in a relatively worse off condition militarily. The PLA has made some improvements in the ability to conduct joint and combined arms warfare, yet it remains qualitatively inferior to India, Russia, Taiwan, and Japan. "For the foreseeable future, China will lack the resources and ability to compete as a military equal with other great powers, much less establish regional domination or become a global superpower."[15] Yet the authors concede that China can destabilize multiple regions with arms sales if necessary to leverage its interests.

According to Nathan and Ross, the image of rogue arms exporter is not accurate. China employs arms sales to raise revenue for modernization and to influence the policy of other nations. In 1980, it defended its decision to sell a nuclear reactor to Algeria by observing that it was in compliance with all International Atomic Energy Agency Commission requirements. In 1988, China delivered the internationally sanctioned CSS-2 ballistic missile to Saudi Arabia to garner revenue and influence the Saudis to break

---

[15]Ibid., 156.

relations with Taiwan. China refuses to commit to the Missile Technology Control Regime (MTCR) to leverage the US on sales of advanced weapons to Taiwan. Its long term assistance program to Pakistan reinforces its relationship with an important regional ally. The authors point out that Chinese arms sales are no different and no more destabilizing than US arms sales to Israel or F-16 sales to Pakistan. In July of 1996, China signed the Nuclear Test Ban Treaty agreement but warned that it would abrogate the treaty if the US deployed a theater ballistic missile defense system in Asia capable of undermining China's second strike capability.[16] China has a long-standing position of supporting nuclear disarmament if the US and Russia did so as well.

Economically, Nathan and Ross point out that each step toward integration with world markets gave greater influence over the Chinese economy to the West, as well as greater dependency on the US market and the dollar. The US trade deficit with China in 1995 was $33.8 billion, exceeding even the Japanese trade imbalance. From the late 1970s to the 1990s, conditional credits from the United Nations Development Program, International Monetary Fund, World Bank, and the Asian Development Bank, as well as aid from other nations, had a direct impact on Chinese internal policies.[17] China links trade to influence the foreign policy of other countries as well. There are economic linkages with the Republic of Korea for coal and with Japan for oil.

The authors note that private capital investment, joint ventures, and foreign direct investment provide the largest source of capital. They assert that in 1994, China received

[16]Ibid., 155.

[17]Ibid., 165.

19

15 percent of all foreign direct investment, second only to the United States, and that China was the largest single aid recipient in the world. They also note that by 1995 almost all sectors of the Chinese economy were open to foreign investment. In 1995, China was the world's tenth largest trader and accumulated a foreign exchange reserve of $75.4 Billion, the fourth largest after Japan, Taiwan, and the US. Additionally, the authors point out that China provides $300 million in international aid per year, primarily to compete with the Republic of China for recognition and political influence. Nathan and Ross conclude by observing that China possesses power that it is only now learning to use. They also point out that the US and China possess mutual interests in economic prosperity; in stability in Asia, Russia, the Korean peninsula, Cambodia, and Pakistan; and in containing Muslim fundamentalism and Japanese militarism.

Another view is provided by Richard Bernstein and Ross H. Munro. In *The Coming Conflict with China*, the authors contend that growing economic and military strength, linked to national ambitions and xenophobic impulses, is making China more aggressive.[18] "China is an unsatisfied and ambitious power, whose goal is to dominate Asia, not by invading and occupying neighboring nations, but by being so much more powerful than they are that nothing will be allowed to happen in East Asia without China's at least tacit consent."[19] They also conclude that "the elements of size, population, and economic resources that ensured its [China's] superpower past will

---

[18]Richard Bernstein and Ross Munro, *The Coming Conflict with China* (New York: Alfred A. Knopf, Inc., 1997).

[19]Ibid., 4.

20

guarantee its superpower future."[20] The growth of power in an aggressive pursuit of interest conforms to China's "historic aggrievement" and "thwarted grandeur." This condition is exacerbated by the demise of the Soviet Union since China no longer requires cooperation with the US as a counterbalance to Soviet Power. The authors observe that communist ideology and its inherent messianic impulses have now been replaced by an aggressive nationalism which is even more dangerous to the region.

The authors point out that the Chinese perceive themselves the victim of a conspiracy of containment led by the US and aimed at preventing China from growing powerful, keeping China weak, without influence, and poor. Evidence of the above is seen in US moves to strengthen security relations with Japan and Australia and in the improvement of relations with India and Vietnam. They also highlight the publication of a popular nationalist, anti-United States manifesto, *China Can Say No,* written by young intellectuals and tacitly supported by the regime.[21] The key points advocated by the book are: fighting back against American cultural and economic imperialism; joining with Russia in an anti-American alliance; boycotting American wheat and other products; demanding compensation for the use of gunpowder, paper, and other Chinese inventions; and a declaration that China is ready to do without most favored nation (MFN) status and ready to impose high import duties on Western goods.

In the debate between engagement and containment, Bernstein and Munro point out the paradox that under Mao, China was feared but weak, but reforms make China

---

[20]Ibid., 20.

[21]Ibid., 48.

21

stronger at the same time the West becomes less fearful of it. They also assert that the post-Deng leadership is weak and playing on nationalism to survive. In this view, China will risk war because "it is in the interest of the governing clique to use external problems as a scapegoat to ensure the survival of the regime."[22] They believe that Chinese goals are to: replace the US as the preeminent superpower in Asia; reduce US influence; prevent Japanese and US containment of China; and to achieve a kind of hegemony which will enable China to influence the foreign policy of all regional actors in the area.[23] According to Bernstein and Munro, Chinese foreign policy is characterized by insecurity, paranoia, arrogance, and the use of bluster, threats, and xenophobic appeals. However, they also believe that China's policy is grounded in realpolitik, where relations with other nations are based upon spheres of influence, balance of power, and struggles for domination.

Bernstein and Munro cite three reasons for skepticism on Chinese public pronouncements of peace: (1) China is now passing into a new phase of history, an era of restored national greatness; (2) China is so large and naturally powerful that it will tend to dominate the region as a matter of policy; and (3) China has pursued initiatives and framed strategic goals that belie claims of modest third world status. Additionally, they note the disparity between Chinese domestic propaganda and statements made to the foreign press. They further state that these elements combine to make a Chinese move toward hegemony virtually inevitable.[24] As concrete manifestations of these

---

[22]Ibid., 48.

[23]Ibid., 11.

[24]Ibid., 53.

developments, the authors cite a litany of perceived Chinese aggressions: the seizure of the Paracel Islands from South Vietnam in 1974; the incursion into Vietnam in 1979; the seizure of Mischief Reef from the Philippines in 1995; and the military show of force against Taiwan during the 1996 crisis in the Taiwan Strait. They also note that in November 1994, while Jiang Zemin visited many countries in Southeast Asia proclaiming Chinese peaceful intentions with respect to the settlement of territorial disputes in the South China Sea, China was building bunkers equipped with radar and satellite dishes on Mischief Reef to support naval operations, while at the same time referring to them as simple fisherman structures. These events are characterized as probing efforts to test the political will of China's neighbors and the United States. Ultimately, according to Bernstein and Munro, China's actions demonstrate a determination to extend power deep into the South China Sea in order to control strategically vital sea routes supporting Japanese, European, and Middle Eastern trade in oil. According to the authors, the recent military and diplomatic policy of China has been aimed at exploiting a maritime geography that would enable China to flank Asia's major sea lanes and trading routes. Additionally, they observe that China has declared the right to regulate navigation through the waters of the South China Sea, though stating it would not exercise that right.

The authors also cite China's alleged attempts to develop a military power-projection capability. They highlight plans to turn Hong Kong's Stone Cutters Island into a naval base, the negotiations with France and the Ukraine on the purchase of an aircraft carrier, the purchase of Soviet IL-76 long-range aircraft, purchases of British and Israeli

23

early-warning and search radars, and attempts to develop an inflight refueling capability to extend the range of combat aircraft.[25] Also discussed is the building of a rail link from Yunnan through Myanmar to the port of Bengal, allegedly to support naval operations in the Indian Ocean. China's military drawdown in the 1980s enabled China to focus on missile, air, naval, and marine power projection and to develop an elite rapid deployment corps of "first troops" capable of amphibious and airborne operations. China also purchased the rights to produce advanced SU-27 multirole aircraft from the Russians and began domestic production in 1995.

With respect to the enigma of Chinese defense expenditures, Bernstein and Munro assert that official Chinese numbers are inaccurate by a factor of ten and believe that when factoring in the revenues of "PLA Incorporated," the budget of the People' Armed Police, and greater relative purchasing power, Chinese defense expenditures approach $87 billion per year, or 30 percent of that of the US.[26] Nevertheless, the authors observe that the essential measure of any country's strength is not absolute power but power relative to others and contend that China's neighbors are weaker. Additionally, the United States' rapid victory over Iraq during the Gulf War caused China to dramatically reevaluate its military capabilities and doctrine, causing a marked interest in developing advanced weapons technologies and in revising doctrine from people's war to fighting modern local wars under high technology conditions in the future. Bernstein and Munro further cite as evidence of Chinese aggressive intent the transfer of nuclear technologies

---

[25]Ibid., 25.

[26]Ibid., 72.

24

to Pakistan, attempts to sell advanced missile technologies to Iran, and the issuance of diplomatic warnings to neighboring countries that they must first consider Chinese interests before the interests of outsiders.[27]

Economically, Bernstein and Munro point out that China is rich in raw materials and that its economy has grown approximately 10 percent per year. They state that China is consciously following a mercantilist economic strategy, stressing exports, technology transfers, capital imports, and barriers to economic competition. In June of 1996, China's trade imbalance with the US was $3.3 billion, exceeding even Japan.[28] They assert that China has two choices: either pursue prosperity via democracy and moderation, seeking participation in the international order and stability, or pursue aggressive policies in defiance of international norms, employing economic leverage to influence the markets and policies of other nations. The authors believe that the latter is the case, stating that China is a corporatist, militarized, nationalist state approximating fascism without the racial nihilism and armed messianism.[29] They cite the "cult of the state" that exists in China, where the party controls all information and demands complete loyalty. The authors also express concern over the relationship between the military and the state in business enterprises, the fact that the army is the most powerful institution in the government, and the existence of a vast security and police system. They believe that an economic downturn combined with rising unfulfilled expectations will result in political

---

[27]Ibid., 20.

[28]Ibid., 26.

[29]Ibid., 61.

instability and increased state repression, at which time China's greater authoritarianism will deflect internal problems externally.

Alastair Johnston, the John L. Loeb Associate Professor of the Social Sciences at Harvard University, provides a third view. He writes in the *Harvard Asia Pacific Review,* "Engaging Myths: Misconceptions about China and its Global Role," that those who debate about the relative merit of engagement or containment operate on the incorrect assumption that China exists and operates outside the international community. He states that China is engaged and involved in the international community as most other states. "China is essentially a status quo major power, being certainly more satisfied with its status and with existing institutions than at any time since 1949."[30] He goes on to state that China is not a rogue state operating in an uncontrolled fashion outside of some fictitious community. On issues, such as arms sales, protectionism, and military modernization, China is only doing what the other major powers do.

Johnston observes that according to the World Bank's 1997 World Development Program, 40 percent of China's gross domestic product (GDP) is involved in trade with other nations, a traditional measure of integration into the global capitalist economy. Additionally, when examining China's participation in universal International Governmental Organizations (IGOs), China is a member of thirty out of thirty-six existing IGOs. This proportion of membership represents 90 percent of US memberships. When weighed against a more critical measure, such as embracing shared

---

[30]Alastair I. Johnston, "Engaging Myths" (Harvard: Harvard Asia Pacific Review); available from http://hcs.harvard.edu/~haprW9/98/johnston.html; accessed 29 September 1998. 5.

international norms with respect to trade, human rights, and arms proliferation, Johnston argues that no such universal norms or objective measures exist. He also observes that though China's economy is not as open as the US, it has made great improvements, with tariffs dropping over 40 percent in the period between 1988 and 1996. With respect to human rights, he readily concedes that China's record is appalling, but also states that despite China's refrain that human rights issues are culturally relative and only within the jurisdiction of sovereign states, China has signed a wide range of international conventions on human rights and supported investigations of violations in South Africa, Cuba, and Afghanistan. As a counterpoint, Johnston also challenges the abstract concept of the existence of international human rights norms by addressing human rights issues in other members of the international community, including the US given its treatment of racial minorities. He goes on to state that "as much as we abhor it, China can and does put together a coalition of states, many of which strongly support free trade and endorse the Chinese view of human rights as stressing community development first."[31] With regard to arms proliferation, Johnston observes that China's sale of ballistic missiles is no more destabilizing than the sale of advanced aircraft by the United States, Europe, and Russia, which are in fact better platforms for delivering weapons of mass destruction than relatively inaccurate Chinese missiles. Johnston concludes that like most other status quo powers, some of China's interests may be accommodated, some may be constrained by positive or negative inducements within international institutions, and others can be transformed through peaceful political and institutional evolution within China itself. His

[31]Ibid., 3.

key point is that "by most measures, the distance between China's behavior and on international normative issues and that of other states . . . are often not as great as the engagers and their critics would have us believe."[32]

Johnston also addresses the concept of the existence of a Chinese strategic culture in his book *Cultural Realism: Strategic Culture and Grand Strategy in Chinese History*.[33] The work focuses on employing historical and cultural explanations (derived from the analysis of *The Seven Military Classics*) for Chinese state behavior to analyze the effect of a Chinese strategic culture on grand strategic choices in history and in the future. He posits that strategic culture is socialized in leaders via classic texts and lends itself to a ranked set of grand strategic preferences in foreign policy. He also argues that the strategic culture can impact policy by narrowing the range of options available to decision makers. Two competing cultures exist. One is the Confucian-Mencian paradigm, which assumes that conflict is aberrant or at least avoidable through the promotion of good government and the coopting and enculturation of external threats. In this model, when force is used, it is done so minimally as a last recourse and in the name of a righteous restoration of moral-political order. It places strategies of accommodation and defense before offensive strategies. The opposing model is what Johnston defines as the parabellum paradigm, which assumes that conflict is a constant feature in human affairs and is largely due to the threatening nature of an adversary and that in this zero-

[32]Ibid., 5.

[33]Alastair I. Johnston, *Cultural Realism: Strategic Culture and Grand Strategy in Chinese History* (Princeton, NJ: Princeton University Press, 1995).

sum context, violence is the most effective means for dealing with an antagonist. This concept is moderated by the Chinese concept of *quan bian*, absolute flexibility, wherein the use of force is only effective if certain strategic conditions are met.[34] Therefore the object of policy is to establish such favorable conditions during periods of weakness, attacking and defending according to opportunity.

Johnston counters what he believes is the contemporary perception of Chinese international behavior which asserts Chinese uniqueness in its defensive and accommodating (Confucian-Mencian) strategic culture. He states that based on his analysis of classic literature, this commonly held misperception is not the model for Chinese international behavior, but that it is rather the parabellum model which is dominant. In this view, security is achieved through superior military preparations, the application of violence, and the destruction of the adversary. According to Johnston, the Confucian-Mencian concept of "not fighting and subduing the enemy" is not borne out by the "frequency and scale of state violence in Chinese history."[35] Of even greater significance to this inquiry, is his argument that in post-1949 China, the use of force appears to have been related to improvements against relative capabilities. Johnston concludes that even though Chinese strategic culture does not differ radically from key elements in the Western realpolitik tradition, in China's case, it is "a long term, deeply

---

[34]Ibid., 249.

[35]Ibid., 254.

rooted, persistent, and consistent set of assumptions about the strategic environment and about the best means for dealing with it."[36]

Richard J. Smith, professor of Asian studies at Rice University employs a similar historic approach, but arrives at different conclusions. In *The Past in China's Present*, he examines the issues of territorial integrity and national sovereignty in China's history, as well as Chinese responses to internal disorder and China's role in East Asia. He addresses how an "appropriate understanding of Chinese history can provide a unified sense of culture and an understanding of the ways ideas, politics, economics, technology, and other factors interact over short periods of time to constitute a relatively stable but still changing civilization."[37] Smith asserts that the influence of the past is an important aspect of the relationship between China's international relations and domestic policies. He points out that China has a several thousand year old set of sociopolitical traditions to draw upon. He also warns of the danger in applying Western social science models and theory to non-Western data. Smith goes on to state, "International relations, as defined in part by international law, is a naturalized, hegemonic discourse that exists today as an artifact of the European global expansion from the 16th century onward," noting that China learned about international law through gunboat diplomacy and extraterritoriality.[38] Even though leaders and governments change, the fundamental dilemmas facing China

---

[36]Ibid., 258.

[37]Richard J. Smith, *The Past in China's Present. An Historical Perspective on China's Contemporary Approach to International Relations* (Rice University); available from http://www.owlnet.rice.edu/~anth220/thepast.html; accessed 9 October 1998.

[38]Ibid., 6.

remain the same. China today is surrounded by powerful neighbors and potential

adversaries, including the United States, Japan, Russia, India, Vietnam, North Korea,

South Korea, and Taiwan.

Smith postulates that historic and consistent patterns of the rise, prosperity,

decline, and fall of successive Chinese dynasties exist in China's history. The

contemporary concern of the Chinese is the same as the historic Confucian concern: the

desire to protect territorial integrity, control of the internal population and preserve

internal order and to gain access to foreign technology while at the same time limiting the

influence of foreign ideas. He concludes that the influences of past examples and

experiences are still very strong in Chinese domestic and foreign policy formulation, and

that it is delusional to view strategy and the nature and uses of forces through an Anglo-

American lens.

In *The Clash of Civilizations and the Remaking of the World Order*, Samuel P.

Huntington argues that Chinese history, culture, traditions, size, economic dynamism, and

self-image "impel it to assume a hegemonic position in East Asia."[39] He states that this

goal is a natural result of rapid economic development and was also reflected in the

histories of other nations which engaged in expansion coincidental with or immediately

following rapid industrialization and economic growth. He also observes that the

emergence of new great powers is always highly destabilizing. However, he also asserts

that, with rare exceptions, Chinese hegemony in East Asia is unlikely to involve

---

[39]Samuel P. Huntington, *The Clash of Civilizations and the Remaking of the World Order* (New York: Touchstone, 1997), 229.

expansion of territory through direct military force. Huntington believes that Chinese hegemony will manifest itself through pressure on other East Asian countries to, in varying degrees, do some or all of the following:

1. Support Chinese territorial integrity, including Tibet, Xinjiang, and the integration of Taiwan

2. Acquiesce in Chinese sovereignty over the South China Sea and possibly Mongolia

3. Generally support China in conflicts with the West over economics, human rights, weapons proliferation, and other issues

4. Accept Chinese military predominance in the region and refrain from acquiring nuclear weapons or conventional forces that could challenge that predominance

5. Adopt trade and investment policies compatible with Chinese interests and conducive to Chinese economic development

6. Defer to Chinese leadership in dealing with regional problems

7. Be generally open to immigration from China

8. Prohibit or suppress anti-China and anti-Chinese movements within their societies

9. Respect the rights of Chinese within their societies, including their right to maintain close relations with their kin and provinces of origin within China

10. Abstain from military alliances or anti-China coalitions with other powers

11. Promote the use of Mandarin as a supplement to and eventually a replacement for English as the Language of Wider Communication in East Asia[40]

Finally, many scholars accept the view of Alvin and Heidi Toffler as expressed in their book *War and Anti-War, Survival at the Dawn of the 21st Century* though for reasons which are unique to China, rather than part of an overarching social phenomena confronting the entire planet, as advanced by the Tofflers. In this view, the future of China will reflect, in the words of General George Yao, Deputy Prime Minister of Singapore, hundreds of "Singapore like city states."[41] This end state will be the result of China's ethnic and cultural diversity, as well as the economic stratification occurring between Beijing and the increasingly independent and commercially prosperous coastal cities.

As demonstrated by the bibliography, many sources were consulted in the formulation of this thesis. However, the author will now briefly address only the most useful sources of literature which formed the foundation of each case study. Of particular interest to researchers and scholars is the Woodrow Wilson International Center for Scholars. The center is under the Division of International Studies headed by Ambassador Robert Hutchings and includes the Cold War International History Project, directed by James G. Hershberg. The stated purpose of the project is to improve scholarly and public understandings of the Cold War's history on the basis of new

---

[40]Ibid., 230-231.

[41]Alvin Toffler and Heidi Toffler, *War and Anti War* (New York: Little, Brown, and Company, 1993), 242.

evidence emerging from the archives of the erstwhile communist block. It aims to transcend regional and linguistic specializations by assembling scholars and sources from all participants in the Cold War, and to serve as a clearing house for new sources and findings. This resource is vital to accessing the latest available primary source correspondence and other material between Mao Tse Tung and Joseph Stalin, as well as other significant officials. New information analyzed by Alexandre Y. Mansourov from the Russian Republic and Chen Jian from the People's Republic of China corroborates the analysis of Allen S. Whiting's prescient arguments on the origins of the Korean War and the motivation of the Chinese in intervening. *Uncertain Partners, Stalin, Mao, and the Korean War*, cowritten by Sergei N. Goncharov, John W. Lewis, and Xue Litai, also provides a detailed analysis and chronology of the key players and events leading up to the Chinese intervention in Korea. These two sources debunk many commonly accepted myths with respect to the inception of the Korean War.

Unfortunately, as a result of the common practice by government security officials of not releasing sensitive material relating to national policy until the passing of several decades, little information is available on the Sino-Indian and Sino-Vietnamese conflicts, though, with the exception of M. Y. Prozumenschikov's article "The Sino-Soviet Conflict, the Cuban Missile Crisis, and the Sino-Soviet Split, October 1962: New Evidence from the Russian Archives." This work, as declared in the title, provides an interesting account of the geopolitical and ideological schism between the Soviet Union and China and of the Soviet reversals in policy on the Sino-Indian border dispute in the context of potential conflict with the US over missiles in Cuba. As time progresses, more

34

details can be expected to be released by government archives, and this site will continue to provide a fascinating insight into the decision-making rationale for both the Soviets and the Chinese.

The most challenging and frustrating case study research effort was that on the Sino-Indian conflict. Much official government information from both China and India is available; however, little independent objective material could be found. The most authoritative objective examination of the conflict can be found in *India's China war*, written by Neville Maxwell. His detailed account examines the origins of the conflict, beginning with British imperial policy in India and continuing through the development of foreign policy by the newly independent India and the new communist Chinese state. One shortfall readily conceded by the author is the availability of Indian sources critical of Indian policy relative to the paucity of sources available to examine the details of Chinese policy formulation during the crisis. Nevertheless, relying on official government documents, candid accounts by former officials, and third party records of the events preceding the conflict, Maxwell's account provides the most objective analysis of the conflict available. His work challenges previously held assumptions with respect to the causes of the conflict and received high praise by Allen S. Whiting, the preeminent Chinese and Asia scholar of the period. Maxwell's analysis and conclusions are also supported by Michael Edwardes' biography on Nehru, *Nehru, a Political Biography*, wherein he ascribes the conflict to Indian intransigence and jingoistic nationalism.

In an attempt to balance Maxwell's and Edwardes' works, this study includes the prevailing Indian perspective of the conflict as represented by Indian Major General D. K.

Palit's book *War in the High Himalaya*. Palit's perspective was from that of the position of Director of Military Operations during the time of the conflict. Consequently, his account primarily addresses the Indian operational aspect of the conflict. However, his first two chapters provide vital insight into the uniquely Indian perspective of the historic origins of the conflict as well as the perspective of the Nehru government. Though at variance with Maxwell over the legitimacy of the McMahon Line and the specific events of the 1914 Simla Conference, Palit corroborates Maxwell's analysis of the roles played by domestic political pressures, misperception, and miscalculation. Unfortunately, other works from the Indian perspective as represented by B. N. Pandey's bibliographic work *Nehru*, and P. C. Chakravarti's book *India's China Policy*, and singularly cite Chinese aggression for the cause of the conflict, without any detailed account of events or analysis to support such conclusions beyond asserting the legality of the McMahon Line.

Much information is available on the Sino-Vietnamese conflict. The case study analysis in this document relies principally on two comprehensive sources: *China's War with Vietnam, 1979* by King C. Chen and *The Breakdown of the Sino-Vietnamese Alliance, 1970-1979*, by Anne Gilks. Chen examines the history of relations between China and Indochina and analyzes the role played by the Chinese leadership, the complexity of the relationship between China, the Soviet Union and Vietnam, and the role played by Kampuchea within Chinese and Vietnamese geopolitical interests. He also attempts to measure the level of the war relative to other conflicts involving the Chinese and to address the factors which caused China to limit its military action against Vietnam.

Gilks' work addresses the Sino-Vietnamese war by analyzing the convergence and divergence of Chinese and Vietnamese regional interests over time and within the context of the triangular relationship between China, Vietnam, and the Soviet Union. Gilks also examines the fundamental disagreements on the perception of superpower threat and of regional power arrangements. Emphasis is placed on the Chinese management of its "prisoners dilemma" in seeking to contain Vietnamese and Soviet ambitions without creating a self-fulfilling prophesy of a "stable marriage" between its two antagonists. Gilks addresses the impact of mutually reinforcing perceptions of threat over Kampuchea, ethnic Chinese in Vietnam, and territorial and maritime disputes, and the resulting insecurity spiral, all of which ultimately culminate the Vietnamese invasion of Kampuchea and China's subsequent punitive war against Vietnam. Chen's and Gilks' works reinforce and complement each other in providing a thorough understanding of the numerous and complicated factors which gave rise to the conflict.

To sufficiently grasp a more holistic understanding of future Chinese intentions and national interests, in addition to the necessity of understanding the relevant factors of each historical case study in conflict, it is also necessary to understand the contemporary issues confronting China and Asia. Though not specifically cited, numerous articles in many outstanding journals, such as *Foreign Affairs, Foreign Policy, Asian Affairs, China Quarterly, the Institute for International Studies, the Center for Strategic and International Studies,* and *the Southeast Economic Review,* feature opposing viewpoints on issues confronting both China and Asia and provide an absolutely vital context in which to assess future Chinese behavior.

CHAPTER 3

KOREA

Rational decision making posits decisions as resulting from a logical assessment of desired goals and available means and as being implemented in a manner calculated to make the gains outweigh the costs.[1]

Allen S. Whiting

On 25 June 1950, the Democratic People's Republic of Korea (DPRK) attacked the Republic of Korea (ROK). ROK and US forces were pushed south into the Pusan Perimeter. On 15 September, General MacArthur conducted an amphibious envelopment at Inchon which forced the North Korean forces to fall back. By 7 October, despite warnings from the newly established People's Republic of China (PRC), US forces crossed the 38th parallel and threatened the survival of the DPRK government. On 14 October Chinese Peoples Volunteers (CPV) began crossing the Yalu and by 27 October, became fully engaged with US and UN forces in a struggle which last almost three years and cost over two and one-half million lives.[2]

This chapter will examine the inception of the war, the motives and roles played by each of the actors, the role played by miscalculation and misperception, the diplomatic signaling, and a general chronology of events leading to Chinese intervention. This section concludes with an analysis of China's decision to intervene, the ramifications of a failure to do so, and the objectives it secured by engaging in a war with the United States and its UN allies.

---

[1]Allen S. Whiting, *China Crosses the Yalu* (California: Stanford University Press, 1960).

[2]Bevin Alexander, *Korea, the First War We Lost* (New York: Hippocrene Books, 1986), 483.

Recently opened Russian archives confirm that the direct cause of the Korean conflict was the unification aims of Kim Il Sung, aided and abetted by Joseph Stalin and consented to by Mao Zedong. What is less clear is the role played by China in the genesis of the war prior to the commitment of Chinese combat forces into Korea. Traditionalists viewed China as playing a key role in planning the war with Stalin. This view lost favor after a RAND study conducted by Allen S. Whiting (Stanford University) was published in 1960 and was confirmed after Russian archives became available to researchers.[3] Revisionists held that China was unaware of plans of Stalin and Kim for invading the South and was manipulated into the war by Stalin, who feared possible Chinese-US collusion. Post-revisionist theory, corroborated by access to Russian archives, suggests that Mao gave tacit approval to Kim and endorsed Stalin's decision, expecting a quick North Korean victory and little US interference. According to the post-revisionists, it was not until the US forces crossed the 38th Parallel to unify the country under the auspices of the UN that China fully committed itself to a conflict that neither China nor the United States wanted.

Given the belligerent rhetoric of the South Korean (ROK) government of Syngman Rhee and the growing provocations along the Ongjin border by ROK police and armed forces in 1949, Stalin feared an attack by South Korea on the North. However, Kim Il Sung increasingly pressured Stalin for permission to liberate the South, assuring him that the requisite revolutionary conditions were present and that the relative strength of the NKPA (North Korean People's Army) would assure a rapid victory. Stalin

---

[3]Whiting.

demurred, citing the relative weakness of the NKPA at the time and the possibility of intervention by the US. It was not until Kim convinced Stalin of North Korea's military readiness that Stalin granted approval. Additional factors contributing to Stalin's change in position included the victory of the Chinese Communists over the Nationalists in December 1949; Soviet detonation of its own atomic bomb in August 1949; the establishment of NATO in Europe; and a perceived weakening of US willingness to involve itself in another Asian war.[4] Also, it could be argued that the US abandoned the Nationalists in China, more important politically and geographically than Korea. Therefore, the US was unlikely to go to war over Korea. Stalin also recognized that the reunifying Korea under a satellite regime would provide Moscow a larger buffer zone on Russia's eastern frontier, a strengthened position against a remilitarized Japan, and the opportunity to test US resolve and draw resources away from Europe.[5]

Stalin was eager to ensure that China was willing to support Kim's move in the event North Korea was unable to defeat an American supported South Korea on its own. Mao was aware of Kim's general intent to ultimately unify Korea and agreed in principle, but believed that conditions were not yet favorable for such action in 1949. Preliminary archival evidence suggests that Mao was unaware of Kim's meeting with Stalin in April 1950, where Stalin gave final approval to Kim to invade the South, pending agreement of Mao. Evgueni Bajanov suggests that Stalin did not consult Mao in advance because he

---

[4]Evgueni Bajanov, *Assessing the Politics of the Korean War, 1949*-1951 (Woodrow Wilson International Center for Scholars; Cold War International History Project Bulletin 6-7); available from Internet http://www.gwu.edu/nsarchive/cwihp.html; accessed on 30 January 1999. 2.

[5]Sergei Goncharov, John Lewis, and Xue Litai, *Uncertain Partners, Stalin, Mao, and the Korean War* (Stanford, CA: Stanford University Press, 1993), 139.

wished to conduct the planning himself, without Chinese interference, and present Mao with a fait accompli.[6]

Stalin no doubt noted the withdrawal of US forces in Korea in 1949 and the exclusion of Korea from publicly identified US security interests by Secretary of State Dean Acheson and President Truman.[7] This perception of a lack of US interest in Korea was again conveyed in April 1950, when Tom Connally, Chairman of the Senate Committee on Foreign Relations publicly stated that Korea was not an indispensable part of US defense strategy and that the communists could overrun Korea whenever they "take a notion" to do so.[8] These events reinforced the perception that, given defense requirements in Europe, the United States was unable and therefore uninterested in committing to the defense of Korea. This offered Kim the opportunity to reunify Korea and achieve another communist victory comparable with Mao's achievement in China. Kim's initiative offered Moscow an opportunity to confront US security interests in Asia through a proxy without risking a costly general war in Europe. Furthermore, the March 1950 Sino-Soviet treaty would serve as a strong deterrent against US intervention in Korea. Nevertheless, Stalin wanted Mao to support Kim's proposal so the Soviet Union itself would not have to openly support the DPRK if the US intervened. Additionally, he

---

[6]Evgueni Bajanov, *Assessing the Politics of the Korean War, 1949*-1951 (Woodrow Wilson International Center for Scholars; Cold War International History Project Bulletin 6-7); available from http://www.gwu.edu/nsarchive/cwihp.html; accessed 30 January 1999. 3.

[7]Edwin P. Hoyt, *The Day the Chinese* Attacked (New York: Paragon House, 1993), 70.

[8]Sergei Goncharov, John Lewis, and Xue Litai, *Uncertain Partners, Stalin, Mao, and the Korean War* (Stanford California: Stanford University Press, 1993), 151.

41

warned Kim that "in the event you [Kim] should get kicked in the teeth, I [Stalin] shall not lift a finger . . . you have to ask Mao for all of the help."[9]

Mao first became aware of a concrete plan to invade the South when he was consulted by Kim in May 1950. Mao then requested additional information from Stalin. According to Bajanov, Stalin informed Mao that the international situation had changed to favor Kim's plan for unification. Mao allegedly concurred, stating that if the Americans interfered, China would help.[10]

Mao's tacit endorsement of Kim's and Stalin's adventurism was given in May, but only after serious consideration. Initially Mao expressed reservations, fearing the likelihood of provoking a US intervention. He further pointed out that he first needed to consolidate the communist victory in China and complete it by liberating Taiwan. Yet China could not object to Korean efforts at unification while simultaneously pursuing its own efforts to liberate Taiwan. Also, Mao secured Soviet support for his invasion of Taiwan, and could not express fears over US intervention in Korea without highlighting the same possibility with respect to Taiwan.[11] In January 1950, Mao did consent to Kim's request to repatriate the 14,000 Korean People's Liberation Army Volunteers (KPLA). As an additional precautionary measure, he redeployed Lin Biao's elite field army from the southeast to the northeast along the Manchurian border in May and June 1950. The maneuver's purpose was to guard the vulnerable Manchurian border against an American,

---

[9]Ibid., 145.

[10]Bajanov, 3.

[11]Goncharov, 146.

South Korean, and Nationalist Chinese counteroffensive in the "unlikely" event Kim would fail, rather than part of a deliberate plan to actively reinforce the North Korean invasion. According to Whiting, no evidence exists of Chinese preparation to enter the war at this early stage.[12] More recent archival evidence corroborates this conclusion, although it does confirm that China was prepared to ensure the survival of the North Korean regime in the event of its defeat by introduced American forces. Though China would clearly benefit from a successful communist unification of the peninsula, such an adventure did not merit the associated risk of China's direct involvement, given the satisfactory nature of the regional status quo from China's perspective. Strategic and ideological considerations of support to the DPRK were subordinated to the requirement of attaining international acceptance and recognition, and gaining a seat in the UN General Assembly. Mao consented to the enterprise given Kim's assurance that the NKPA would defeat the South before the US had time to react and without assistance from the Chinese. Archival information in fact demonstrates that Kim had deliberately concealed the operational details of his attack, including its timing, from China. Soviet war supplies were shipped to North Korea over more vulnerable sea routes rather than via secure rail lines through China to deny China information on Kim's plans.[13]

The Communist Chinese focus in 1950 was on consolidating the victory over Chiang Kai-shek's Nationalists and rebuilding the nation after decades of civil strife and war with the Japanese. Economic difficulties, industrial rebuilding, agricultural reform,

---

[12]Whiting, 45.

[13]Goncharov, 153.

and internal security problems combined to concentrate efforts internally. China's interest in Korea was limited and defined only in terms of relationships with other countries. No ambassador was posted to the DPRK until well into 1950. After two months the ambassador was recalled, leaving only a charge d'affairs in place.[14] Only Tibet and Taiwan remained issues requiring military redress. The failure of the Marshall Mission to reconcile communist and nationalist differences (aimed at strengthening China to counter balance the Soviet Union) and the excesses of the Kuomantang resulted in a general withdrawal of the US from the Chinese civil war and resignation to the "inevitable" loss of Taiwan to the communists. Likewise, neither the British nor India were in a position to halt the planned pacification of Tibet. Furthermore, Mao realized that he was now competing with Kim for Soviet military support. Beyond Tibet and Taiwan, the Chinese anticipated no military commitments in 1950 and consequently focused on demobilizing the PLA to transfer its associated capital costs to economic development, and on redirecting the army to agricultural and construction tasks.[15]

This situation changed on 27 June 1950 when the US misinterpreted Kim's attack as part of a Soviet and Chinese conspiracy to challenge US containment policy and consequently placed the US 7th Fleet in the Taiwan Strait to block a perceived greater communist offensive in Asia. Additionally, Truman neutralized Taiwan until the final settlement of a peace treaty with Japan or when the issue was resolved by the UN. Secretary of State Acheson believed Kim's invasion was part a communist offensive to

---

[14]Whiting, 44.

[15]Ibid., 19.

44

secure the immediate objectives of Korea, Indochina, Burma (Myanmar), the Philippines and Malaya, and medium range objectives of securing Hong Kong, Indonesia, Siam (Thailand), India, and Japan.[16] The hawkish Republican members of Congress and pro-Nationalist Chinese bloc applied political pressure on the Truman administration to act aggressively in responding to the communist threat. To the Chinese, these actions confirmed that Truman's statement of 5 January 1950 (pledging the US had no interest in the Chinese civil war or in supporting the Chiang Kai-shek regime) was a lie intended to deceive them. Now China's strategic national goal of regaining Taiwan and completing the destruction of the Nationalists and Chiang Kai-shek became inextricably linked with the North Korean defeat of the American forces in Korea. The Chinese believed that a North Korean victory would cause the US to withdraw from Asia in general and Taiwan in particular.[17] China's interest clearly centered on Taiwan and not Korea. China perceived the United States was using Korea as an excuse to reinforce the US military presence in the region and to aid the Nationalist regime on Taiwan. "Chinese security and territorial integrity thus became tied closely to the fortunes of the North Koreans."[18]

Chinese apprehension and suspicion of the United States was founded upon what it perceived as America's rehabilitation and rearmament of its traditional foe, Japan, and America's implacable hostility to communism. This view was reinforced by the attempts of the US to unilaterally establish a separate peace treaty with Japan independent of

---

[16]Rosemary Foot, *The Wrong War* (Ithica, NY: Cornell University Press, 1985), 64.

[17]Whiting, 65.

[18]Foot, 66.

Russia and China. China also viewed NATO's (North American Treaty Organization) establishment as a precursor to a similar anticommunist (anti-China) arrangement in Asia. American assistance to South Korea, efforts to block China's admission into the United Nations, recognition and support of Chiang Kai-shek's Republic of China, military aid to the Philippines and to the French in Indochina and the British in Malaya also led China to view of the US as an aggressive imperialist power bent on dominating Asia. China's decision on 14 February 1950 to engage the Soviet Union in the Treaty of Friendship, Alliance, and Mutual Assistance (ratified on 30 September) was intended to deter a possible attack by a Japanese-American coalition. Mao's "lean to one side" announcement (addressing the need of China to align with the Soviets against the West) was born of the necessity to form a united front against perceived American and Japanese imperialism. As early as 1949, Mao feared the United States would intervene on behalf of the Nationalists during the PLA's final push to seize Shanghai.[19]

To understand these perspectives and motivations, one must first understand the region's geography and history and the strategic context. According to Whiting, China possesses "xenophobic attitudes and expansionist tendencies" which manifest themselves during respective periods of strength and weakness.[20] China's concept of national boundaries and territorial sovereignty goes back to the Chinese perception of itself as the Middle Kingdom. These boundaries have changed countless times and were relatively

---

[19]Mun Su Park, *The International Dimensions of the Korean War: Geopolitical Realism, Misperception, and Post Revisionism* (Buffalo, New York: University of New York, UMI Dissertation Services, 1993), 171.

[20]Whiting, 1.

unsurveyed. This condition was heightened in the nineteenth century by French pressure

in Indochina; British pressure in Burma (Myanmar) and India; Russian pressure in

Xinjiang, Mongolia, and Manchuria; and Japanese pressure in Korea, Manchuria, the

Ryukyu Islands, and Taiwan.[21] Compounding China's sovereignty problems were

Western commercial interests and ideological penetration, which, beginning in the 1840s

and extending into the 1920s, codified in a series of unequal treaties granting foreign

extraterritoriality though consular jurisdiction and concessions. After 1949, elements of

China's large and ethnically varied population continued to resist communist

indoctrination and control. These factors combined to cause China to fear the intentions

of outside powers, particularly Japan, the US, and Russia.

Mao's adaptation of Marxist-Leninist thought influenced this xenophobia and

resentment by imparting a philosophical and revolutionary framework to China's historic

and contemporary problems. Leninism's concept of inevitable conflict with imperialism

and Mao's denial of a neutral "third path"[22] dovetailed with China's historic experience to

generate forces which culminated in the expansion of the Korean war. Other factors, like

China's externally imposed and internally self-inflicted isolation from the world and its

uncritical acceptance of the communist model of world affairs, also contributed to this

problem.

The US perceived that Kim Il Sung's invasion of the South was a Moscow

inspired test of Western resolve, not unlike Iran in 1946, Greece in 1947, and Berlin in

---

[21]Ibid., 2.

[22]A viable alternative to capitalism or Marxism.

1948-49.[23] These events combined to create an image of a monolithic communist power, directed by Moscow, and aimed at world domination. The experience of Munich and World War II reinforced a distinct US propensity to reason by analogy and equate negotiation with weakness.[24] This interpretation of events was understandably conceived at the genesis of the cold war. Its essence was captured in the Truman doctrine. NSC 68, one of the fruits of George Kennan's 1947 "X" article, defined an international environment wherein the Soviets would conduct "proxy wars of aggression" and required the US to draw a line containing communist aggression.[25] A failure to do so would encourage communist aggression. This logic reflected a misapplication of the Munich experience and the failures of appeasement. It would dominate and limit the American approach to policy during much of the cold war. Some analysts hypothesized that Kim's attack was a distraction to lure US forces to Asia, away from the "real" communist war aims in Europe. This mentality was exemplified by Senator Joseph Macarthy, who accused the Truman administration of harboring known communists and being soft on international communism's designs for global domination. This, in turn, resulted in the purge from the State Department of knowledgeable China experts who had previously criticized Chiang Kai-shek's Nationalist regime for corruption and brutality and had presented a more nuanced view of communism in Asia. Consequently, errors in interpreting events in China and Northeast Asia were compounded. Influential voices in

---

[23]Whiting, 3.

[24]Foot, 44.

[25]Ibid., 62.

the United States Congress, already dissatisfied with the Truman administration's foreign policy program, condemned the passive nature of containment and called for aggressive action.[26] The recent "fall of China" to the communists and Soviet explosion of an atomic weapon only heightened US insecurity and anxiety. Stalin and Kim, seeing the shift in public support toward an activist US policy in Asia and the attendant demands to build up US military strength in the region, decided they had to act decisively in Korea before such policies could be adopted and implemented.

Korea's significance to the US policy was not geostrategic but psychological. The US felt compelled to react strongly in order to demonstrate credibility to European allies and resolve to the communist foe. The day after North Korea's invasion, on 26 June 1950, the United States proposed a resolution to the United Nations Security Council (UNSC) calling for the immediate cessation of hostilities and the withdrawal of North Korean forces to the 38th Parallel. The resolution was adopted 9-0 with one abstention (Yugoslavia) and one key absence: the Soviet representative Jacob Malik, who was boycotting the UNSC over its refusal to admit the PRC into the General Assembly.

In July, the Indian government initiated a resolution to mediate the conflict and proposed to admit China to the General Assembly and the return of the Soviet Ambassador Jacob Malik to the Security Council. On 1 August, Malik returned to the Security Council and resumed his duties as the rotating President. Concurrently, General MacArthur traveled to Taipei and, issued a joint communiqué with Generalissimo Chiang Kai-shek, announcing a complete "harmony of aims in the region." Chiang proclaimed,

---

[26]Ibid., 35.

49

"now that we can again work closely together with our old comrades in arms, victory was assured." MacArthur reciprocated with assurances of "effective military coordination between Chinese and American forces." This further heightened China's fears of a US-Japanese-Nationalist coalition.[27]

That same day, Kuo Mojo, Chairman of the Chinese World Peace Foundation, made a public speech in Beijing calling on all Chinese to "oppose American imperialism's aggression and to use practical actions to come forward to support the Korean people's just struggle."[28] The PLA chief Chu Teh also delivered a declaration of support for North Korea in its "just war to oppose American aggression."[29] On 4 August, Malik introduced a resolution to invite representatives of the PRC and both Koreas to discuss the conflict, end hostilities, and withdraw all foreign troops. However, United Nations military success in holding and reinforcing the Pusan perimeter and the possibility of conducting a successful counteroffensive emboldened Truman and the UN General Assembly, and the measure was defeated. On 10 August, Warren Austin, American Ambassador to the United Nations, stated that the UN had a "moral obligation" to reunify the Korean peninsula.[30] On 11 August, the United Kingdom introduced a measure to make discussion and withdrawal of foreign troops contingent upon a North Korean withdraw north of the 38th parallel. This proposal was endorsed by India on 14

---

[27]Dean Acheson, *The Korean War* (New York: W. W. Norton and Company, Inc., 1971), 43.

[28]Edmund O. Clubb, *20th Century* China, 3rd edition (New York: Columbia University Press, 1978), 339.

[29]Ibid., 338.

[30]Foot, 69.

August. On 17 August, Austin reiterated that the object of the United Nations was total victory over the North Koreans and unifying the peninsula under UN auspices. On 20 August, Zhou En-lai cabled the United Nations to endorse Malik's resolution and demand a seat at the negotiating table. The message pointedly noted that "the Chinese people cannot be but most concerned about the solution of the Korea question."[31] Malik also warned that the complete reunification of the peninsula by force would expand the war. On 26 August China's *World Culture* claimed the American action in Korea "seriously threatens the security of China in particular. . . . It is impossible to solve the Korean problem without the participation of its closest neighbor, China."[32] These rapid events were inflamed by a press release from General MacArthur which, contrary to current American policy at the time, argued the strategic importance of Taiwan to the United States and the necessity of preventing its falling into the hands of a "hostile power."

On 15 September, MacArthur's successful amphibious landing at Inchon and pursuit of retreating North Korean forces toward the 38th parallel rapidly brought the question of advancing beyond the 38th parallel into North Korea in sharp focus for all parties. Special advisor to the State Department John Foster Dulles publicly advocated the use of force to unify the entire peninsula. Of even greater alarm to the Chinese, the US Congress and the media publicly debated pushing the war into Manchuria, and General MacArthur advocated preemptive strikes against China and the restoration of

---

[31]William Manchester, *American Caesar, Douglas MacArthur, 1880-1964* (Boston: Little, Brown, and Company, 1978), 58.

[32]Whiting, 70.

Chiang Kai-shek, on the mainland.[33] On 19 September, the UN General Assembly

defeated India's proposal to admit China into the United Nations. On 25 September, K.

M. Panikkar, the Indian Ambassador to China, met with PLA General Nieh Jung-chen,

who stated that the Chinese people "did not intend to sit back with folded hands" and let

the Americans come up to their border.[34] This message was subsequently transmitted by

Panikkar to the British government who then forwarded it to the United States.

On 29 September, despite George Kennan's objections over fears of provoking the

Soviets into entering the war, Truman approved NSC 81/1 authorizing General

MacArthur to conduct ground operations north of the 38th parallel.[35] Moscow's failure to

strongly object only emboldened the administration. Secretary of Defense George C.

Marshall sent a message to MacArthur stating that he wanted the general to feel

unhampered strategically and tactically to proceed North of the 38th Parallel. The

Chinese could no longer ignore events in the American dominated UN American

congressional rhetoric, media coverage of MacArthur's belligerent views, and the

increasing violations of Chinese airspace and territorial sovereignty. Chinese propaganda

no longer employed the passive term *fan tui* in pledging resistance to American

aggression but now employed the active term *kang-yi*, previously used in exhorting action

against the Japanese and Nationalists.[36] On 30 September, the Sino-Soviet Treaty was

[33]Edwin P. Hoyt, *The Day the Chinese Attacked* (New York: Paragon House, 1993), 74.

[34]Joseph C. Goulden, *The Untold Story of the Korean* War (New York: New York Times Books, 1982), 281.

[35]Foot, 73.

[36]Whiting, 98.

ratified. Chou En-lai publicly stated, "The Chinese people cannot supinely tolerate foreign aggression, and cannot allow imperialists recklessly to aggress against their own neighbor, and disregard it."[37] That same day, North Korea forwarded to Stalin a message requesting direct military assistance from the Soviet Union or volunteer units of China and other "Socialist Democracies." Stalin responded only by providing additional tactical advice, withdrawing the Soviet representatives from Pyongyang, preparing to evacuate Kim's regime from North Korea, and pressuring the Chinese to enter the conflict.[38]

On 1 October 1950, Stalin sent Mao a message requesting that China move five to six divisions to support the North Koreans. China was already upset over Kim's failure to keep the Chinese informed of the military situation on the ground and for failing to heed Chinese advice to establish a strong defense around Inchon and other ports to prevent an envelopment by American amphibious forces. On the advice of Zhou Enlai and Lin Biao, Mao initially declined to honor his previous commitments, stating that China's armed forces were not strong enough to counter US forces. He also stated that such an event would undermine China's domestic reconstruction plans and could even drag the Soviets into the war.[39] Mao suggested the Koreans accept conventional defeat and continue the fight a guerrilla war. Nevertheless, China did convey to Soviet Ambassador Roshchin that if American forces crossed the 38th parallel, China would enter the conflict.[40]

---

[37]Clubb, 339.

[38]Bajanov, 5.

[39]Ibid., 6.

[40]Ibid., 5.

On 2 October, Soviet Foreign Minister Vyshinsky introduced a cease fire resolution as a counter proposal for the US resolution on complete unification. The Soviets called for the same actions as the failed Indian proposal but also included provisions for all-Korea elections to a national assembly, a joint North-South Korean commission to govern in the interim, observation by an election commission including representatives of states bordering Korea, economic assistance, and the admission of a reconstituted Korean state into the UN. Whiting thought the initiative significant because "a concession on this point (national elections--previously objected to by the Soviets which resulted in the formal division of the country in 1948) suggested a willingness to compromise, particularly since the preponderance of the population lay in the South."[41] Nevertheless, the initiative was defeated in the General Assembly, led by the United States, which had grown overconfident in light of the rapid advances taking place on the battlefield. Even without defeat by the General Assembly, such a proposal would have had little chance of success given the intransigence of both Korean governments.

Also on 2 October, shortly after midnight local time in Beijing, Zhou Enlai summoned Panikkar to deliver an important message: If the US crossed the 38th parallel, China would be forced to intervene. South Korean forces could cross, but US forces would be resisted.[42] He also conveyed Chinese interest in a peaceful settlement. This message was also forwarded to the British and US governments. After Panikkar transmitted the warnings, Washington received additional corroborative reports from

---

[41]Whiting, 112.

[42]Goulden, 281.

neutral channels and from American embassies in Moscow, Stockholm, London, Rangoon, and New Delhi.[43] These messages stated that China had no choice but to fight, "even if war with the US would set China back fifty years." Otherwise, China would "forever be under US control." The Chairman of the Joint Chiefs of Staff (CJCS) General Omar Bradley and Secretary of State Dean Acheson dismissed these threats as a bluff. Allen Kirk, the US ambassador to Moscow, expressed surprise that such a message was not conveyed directly to the UN or the US.[44] James R. Wilkinson, American Counsel General to Hong Kong, dismissed the warnings as "saber rattling."[45] The Central Intelligence Agency estimate concluded that China would not intervene because China "undoubtedly feared the consequence of war with the US" and that their domestic programs "were of such magnitude that the regime's entire domestic program and economy would be jeopardized by the strains."[46] General Willoughby, MacArthur's senior intelligence officer supported these views, calling the Chinese diplomatic messages "propaganda" and "diplomatic blackmail." Only the British expressed concern over the reports.

On 1 October, ROK forces pushed into North Korea. On 5 October, Stalin replied to Mao's refusal to intervene. Stalin argued that Chinese involvement would cause the defeat of the United States and at the same time resolve the Taiwan issue. He also stated

---

[43]Whiting, 109.

[44]Goulden, 282.

[45]Ibid., 282.

[46]Ibid., 284.

55

that if Chinese intervention resulted in an escalation of the war activating the Sino-Soviet treaty, "let it take place now rather than a few years later, when the United States and Japan will possess a military spring-board on the continent in the form of Rhee's Korea."[47] While making bold statements in an attempt to maneuver Mao into saving North Korea, Stalin himself was adeptly preparing to abandon his position and cut his losses. On 6 October, Zhou Enlai cabled the United Nations, protesting that the US proposed resolution to unify Korea was illegal and that the impending advance of UN soldiers into North Korea threatened Chinese interests. Zhou stated, "the PRC would never be afraid to oppose an aggressive enemy."[48] By 7 October, the UN General Assembly voted to support the US resolution to unify all of Korea. Zhou immediately denounced the resolution as illegal, reiterating that American soldiers were menacing Chinese security and that the Chinese would not stand idly by.[49] The UN countered that it would "fully support" the Manchurian border and to that end a resolution was introduced to the Security Council pledging "full protection of Chinese and Korean interests in the security zone."[50] The US State Department further stated that the US had no "ulterior design in Manchuria" and Truman declared that the US had no intention of extending the war into China. No one considered the impact of the loss of US credibility (from the Chinese

---

[47]Bajanov, 6.

[48]John F. O'Shaughnessy, *The Chinese Intervention in Korea: An Analysis of Warning* (Defense Intelligence Agency: Masters of Strategic Studies Thesis, 1985), 27.

[49]Manchester, 582.

[50]Ibid., 600.

point of view) given its policy reversals in Taiwan and in the UNSC. No effort to consider alternative courses of action in light of Chinese warnings was made.

That same day, the US 1st Cavalry Division crossed the 38th Parallel and propelled China into the conflict. In Beijing, after weighing competing arguments regarding intervention during an emergency session of the Politburo, Mao reversed his position, deferring to the arguments of Gao Gang and Peng Dehuai, who reasoned that American occupation of all of Korea would pose a permanent and mortal danger to the Chinese revolution.[51] Mao replied to Moscow that he would intervene, though not immediately. He also made intervention conditional on Soviet military aid and Stalin's meeting with the two principal Chinese opponents to intervention: Zhou Enlai and Lin Biao.[52]

Stalin received Zhou and Lin on 9 October. Zhou outlined the ways in which China lacked adequate capital resources, weapons, and transportation to intervene at this stage, pointed out that China's own domestic opposition was not yet pacified, and that the United States might declare war on China, giving rise to reactionary forces within China.[53] Stalin countered that the Soviet Union was in an even worse position, having just fought the Second World War, that the Soviet-North Korean border was too narrow to support massive troop movements, and that US imperialism was weakened

---

[51]Bajanov, 6.

[52]Alexandre Mansourov, *Stalin, Mao, Kim and China's Decision to Enter the Korean War, September 16-October 15, 1950: New Evidence from Russian Archives* (Woodrow Wilson International Center for Scholars; Cold War International History Project Bulletin 6-7), 13; available from http://www.gwu. edu/nsarchive/cwihp.html; accessed 30 January 1999.

[53]Ibid., 15.

strategically because it could not rely on other imperial forces which had also been weakened as a result of the last war. Zhou remained unconvinced.

What happened next remains in dispute. Goncharov, Xue, and Lewis assert that Stalin then reversed himself and suggested that both China and the Soviets withdraw the remainder of Kim's regime and the NKPA to sanctuaries in China, to be rebuilt and retrained for the later liberation of Korea, abandoning North Korea to the United States.[54] Shocked by this abrupt and undesirable alternative, Zhou inquired if Stalin could provide China with weaponry and air cover if China elected to intervene. Stalin replied affirmatively and Zhou and Lin departed, seeking further instructions from Mao. Mansourov disputes this account as fiction, stating that Stalin reiterated his willingness since July to provide China with air cover if Mao sent troops to Korea.[55] On 11 October, Zhou reportedly cabled Mao that Stalin did not object to China's decision not to intervene in Korea, reigniting the debate in Beijing over the relative merits of Chinese intervention. Consequently, according to Mansourov, when Zhou and Lin returned, they entered the debate and attempted to prevent China from assuming the burden of saving the North Korean regime by falsely stating that Stalin refused to provide the air support necessary for a successful Chinese intervention. Regardless of which account is accurate, ultimately Mao, Peng Dehuai, and Gao Gang's arguments for intervention carried the day. Shortly thereafter, the Associated Press news wire carried reports of Chinese columns crossing the Yalu.

---

[54]Goncharov, Lewis, and Lita.

[55]Mansourov, 16.

Beyond the repatriation of KPLA soldiers in May and June, and shifting of Lin Biao's army to Manchuria, no evidence exists to support claims that China militarily assisted the North Korea prior to U.N. forces crossing the 38th parallel.[56] However, once US forces crossed the parallel, China's strategic security concerns became paramount. Taiwan was no longer the greatest issue at stake. The Chinese perceived the US occupation of all of Korea as a direct threat to Manchuria and the US reoccupation of Taiwan as a direct threat to Shanghai.[57] History could be seen repeating itself. The Chinese expected the US would exploit any pretext to invade China. Indeed, China's world view and communist ideology almost made this unlikely potentiality a self-fulfilling prophesy. The more aggressive China became, the more aggressive the United States became. Each party to the conflict began attributing responses to external problems as coming from the internal nature of the opposing antagonist. Each side succumbed to the "mirror image" of its own aggressive behavior.

Allen Whiting asserts that the Chinese entry into the war was "a belated intervention decided on reluctantly, as a last resort, rather than a carefully premeditated intervention." This assumes that China's actions were rational, if not correct, in the context of the strategic environment in which it was operating. China's decision to intervene was predicated upon preserving the DPRK regime as a buffer state in the path of historic invasion routes into Manchuria, rather than on preserving the DPRK for its own sake. China's war aims were to preempt US momentum from carrying the war into

---

[56]Park, 191.

[57]Hoyt, 80.

Manchuria and China proper, a legitimate concern given the context of events and China's previous experiences with foreign powers. Based on the corroborating evidence from Russian archives and Mansourov's later analysis, Whiting correctly hypothesized that China's strategic interests compelled it to act decisively once the US crossed the 38th Parallel to destroy the DPRK and reunite the country. He states the primary Chinese goal was to reverse the course of US-Japanese relations, which was viewed as a emerging imperialist coalition aimed at China.

Mao's decision to intervene was based on his ideological belief that conflict with imperialism was inevitable and that the cost of acquiescing to US aggression was greater than the cost of going to war. China's perspective was developed in the context of US support for rearming Japan, support for a separate peace treaty, and the use of Japanese facilities and personnel as a base of operations for war in Korea. Additionally, China observed the US supporting "reactionary" regimes suppressing national liberation movements, all of which were being supported or encouraged by China in its self appointed role as the leader of national liberation in Asia. China was not capable of seeing the aggressive American response to the Korean conflict as anything other than a "premeditated offensive design" aimed at China, rather than a defensive reaction. In China's view, total UN victory in Korea would facilitate an American, Japanese, and Korean alignment, posing a grave threat to China. "Korea, as in the past, was less important in itself than for its relationship with other countries."[58]

---

[58]Whiting, 151.

According to Whiting, China's motive for intervening lay in recognizing its own internal and external weakness, and the strategic necessity of preemptively fighting a hostile power in Korea rather than in China. "China's xenophobia, assumptions about the inevitability of conflict, limited information, and acceptance of own propaganda contributed to a highly hostile and suspicious view of the noncommunist world in general and the United States in particular."[59] Therefore, China's decision to intervene was based on "objective vulnerabilities and subjective anxieties" rather than aggression and expansionist aims. China's decision to enter the war was the understanding that the outcome of the Korean War had ramifications for its vital domestic and international interests.[60] Chinese warnings on 20 August and 2 October had been conveyed clearly, but were summarily rejected by the US. Only the British took these warnings seriously, but their concerns were calmed by Acheson, who believed that the Soviet Union would not risk general war and that China would not jeopardize gaining a seat in the UN General Assembly.[61]

US miscalculation can be attributed to multiple factors like the sustained but nuanced Chinese propaganda preceding the serious warnings and the perceived failure of the Chinese to act during the more advantageous periods of US vulnerability at Pusan or Inchon. The absence of diplomatic relations since October 1949 contributed to a major

---

[59]Ibid., 159.

[60]Chen Jian, *China's Road to the Korean War: the making of the Sino-American Confrontation* (New York: Columbia University Press, 1994).

[61]Hoyt, 80.

lack of understanding of Chinese interests.[62] Additionally, the US was unable to conceive that China would challenge the US and accept the inherent risks of intervention. Finally, the US erroneously believed that China could not or would not act independently of the Soviet Union.

Additional factors in the dismissing K. M. Panikkar's warnings lay in Washington's assessment of Panikkar as emotional, unstable, and strongly biased toward Mao.[63] Acheson regarded the warning as a bluff and countered that greater risk was incurred by showing hesitation and timidity than by responding boldly. Dean Rusk believed that if China wanted to intervene, it would have do so at a more propitious time. The Soviet attempt at mediating a cease fire and peace agreement on 4 August seemed to demonstrate a vulnerability which the US was eager to exploit.

The false assumptions made in arriving at these erroneous conclusions were : (1) China's interests were not threatened; (2) China was too focused on consolidating its gains internally; (3) China would not risk its objective of gaining a seat in the United Nations; and (4) that China would require Soviet assistance which would not be offered at the risk of a general war and not be desired at the necessary cost of further Soviet encroachment in Manchuria. The United States was too preoccupied with measuring Soviet responses to policy to recognize China's legitimate security interests or pronouncements. No attempt to analyze the situation from the Chinese perspective was made. George Kennan stated, in retrospect, "Chinese Communism was only of

---

[62]Ibid., 74.

[63]Foot, 79.

62

potentially grave significance as a possible adjunct to Soviet politico-military power" and that "the direct cause of Chinese intervention was the US disregard for Chinese warnings not to cross the 38th parallel. . . . China was compelled to ensure [its] survival."[64]

The belief that the Chinese would not attack was based on a zero sum perspective that if China wished to intervene it would have done so previously. It assumed that China would only intervene for aggressive, offensive reasons and failed to consider why China might be compelled to attack for defensive reasons, like the specter of a hostile power adjacent to Manchuria, a traditional invasion route to China. China was politically and militarily unprepared for war in 1950. The failure to act at a more opportune time demonstrates that China was not interested in offensively challenging Western spheres of influence.[65]

This chapter clearly has shown that China attempted to convey its security interests to the United States through multiple channels. Both the US and the UN heard China's specific warnings, but did not understand them. They failed to give China credibility, not because of Chinese deception, but out of arrogance and ignorance. Though the lack of diplomatic recognition contributed to problems of understanding, this was not the proximate cause of the expansion of the conflict. China's paranoia and ideological dogma contributed to the conflict as well. Yet, had the UN halted at the 38th parallel, Chinese security interests would not have been threatened to the point that it was compelled to go to war. Strategically, China had little alternative, even if it believed that

---

[64]Park, 171.

[65]Only after Mao found it necessary to intervene did he consider retaking the entire peninsula rather than merely reestablishing the prewar boundaries.

the US would not continue the war beyond the Yalu. Such a scenario was not out of the realm of possibility given the military hubris of MacArthur and the political pressure on President Truman. Given China's internal vulnerabilities immediately after the civil war, it was in China's security interest to intervene to ensure the survival of the DPRK as a buffer state. This realist perspective is critical in analyzing China's behavior in the years since 1950 and in formulating assessments of China's behavior in the future.

Like the West, China's experience in the Korean War had a profound impact on its world view and unfortunately reinforced its misperceptions about to the outside world. The more positive result of the conflict was China's subsequent understanding that recognition and engagement via the "third way" was critical to making its interests known and felt during the period of continued isolation by the West, thereby mitigating misperception and miscalculation on the part of itself and its antagonists. Yet, because of China's resolute action, it would never again be ignored or dismissed by the US. Despite the price paid in Chinese blood and treasure, its war aims were achieved and served as a strong reminder of China's determination to defend its interests. China would be recognized as an independent and sovereign state with its own national and security interests, rather than merely another satellite of the Soviet Union. This new reality would shortly become apparent not only to the US but even more so to the Soviet Union.

CHAPTER 4

INDIA

> So solidly built into our consciousness is the concept that China is
> conducting a rapacious and belligerent foreign policy, that
> whenever a dispute rises in which China is involved, she is
> instantly assumed to have provoked it. All commentaries, news
> reports, and scholarly interpretations are written on the basis of this
> assumption. The cumulative of this only further reinforces the
> original hypothesis so that it is used again the next time with even
> greater effect.[1]

Felix Greene

The experiences shared by China and the West after the Korean war served only

to reinforce the mistaken assumptions held by each. China's next external conflict was

born in the fog of this environment but its inception lies in India's colonial past. This

chapter will attempt to outline the inconsistent and ambiguous development of the border

separating India and China, the legacy of British India left to independent India, the role

of nationalism in Indian foreign policy, the strategic context of the dispute, the

perceptions of each power, and the failed efforts of diplomacy to achieve a peaceful

settlement.

To understand the 1962 Sino-Indian border conflict it is necessary to examine its

historic roots. Geographically, the primary focus of the dispute was the Ladakh, a

Himalayan valley of the uppermost Indus River 12,000 feet above sea level. Politically

and culturally, it had been part of Tibet, loyal to Lhasa, though intermittently control was

also exercised by semiautonomous warlords. Tibet, in turn, was understood to be under

---

[1]Neville Maxwell, *India's China War* (New York: Doubleday and Company, 1972), 258.

the suzerainty of China by both Britain and Russia. In 1834, a Dogra Sikh warlord

unsuccessfully attempted to invade Tibet from India. By 1842, the Dogras and Tibet

signed a nonaggression treaty without establishing a clear frontier border, leaving a

mountainous no-man's land between the two kingdoms.[2] The English recognized the

local Dogra warlord as the Maharajah of Jammu and Kashmir in 1846. The Treaty of

Amritsar, forbade any territorial expansion without British consent. This established

British responsibility for the territories of Kashmir's northeastern boundaries adjacent to

Tibet and Xinjiang.

Kashmir's traditional northern border was regarded as lying along the Mustagh-

Karakorum mountain range, extending eastward to the Karakorum Pass, and then taking a

sharp turn southeast and forming the divide between the Aksai Chin and the Ladakh.[3]

This mountain range forms a natural watershed between India and Central Asia.

Consequently, Britain informed China via the viceroy in Canton of the British concept of

delimitation and attempted to establish a formal boundary recognized by China. The

Chinese in turn replied that "The borders of Ladakh and Tibet have been sufficiently and

distinctly fixed, so it would be best to adhere to this ancient arrangement and it will prove

far more convenient to abstain from any additional measures for fixing them."[4]

Consequently, the British boundary commission was unable to demarcate the terrain

between Pangong Lake and the Karakorum mountain range, labeling the area as "terra

---

[2]Maxwell, 11.

[3]D. K. Palit, *War in the Himalaya: The Indian Army in Crisis, 1962* (New York: St. Martin's Press, 1991), 22.

[4]Maxwell, 12.

incognita," given its rugged character and lack of inhabitants.[5] Beyond this range to the northeast lies the Aksai Chin or "Desert of White Stones" and the Kunlun mountains between Xinjiang in the north and Tibet in the south (see figure 1). This area would become the center of the Sino-Indian dispute. Despite the British prohibition on expansion, Kashmiri forces advanced beyond the Karakorum mountains to the slopes of the Kunlun mountains, occupying Shahdula. According to Indian versions of history, the Chinese were too occupied by a Muslim rebellion in Xinjiang to respond, and therefore both the Chinese and the British tacitly accepted the Kunlun Maintains as the boundary between British India and China, though no steps were taken to officially delimit the border in such a manner.[6] By the middle of the nineteenth century, both Britain and Russia viewed Tibet with interest. In 1860, Russia exploited the lack of Chinese control and unrest on another frontier by annexing Chinese territory in the east above the Amur River and northeast of the Ussuri River, establishing the port of Vladivostock and cutting China off from the Sea of Japan. China was forced to accept the loss of these territories in the Treaties of Aigun (1858) and Beijing (1860). China's experience with Imperial Russia had imparted a painful lesson: "never to negotiate boundary settlements from a position of weakness."[7] This lesson would be recalled and heeded by China one century later. Fearing Russian encroachments from the north toward the Hindu Kush and Karakorum mountains (and India), the British made several unsuccessful attempts to

---

[5]Ibid., 13.

[6]Palit, 25.

[7]Maxwell, 17.

Figure 1. China-India Border: Wesern Sector detailing Aksai Chin and Respective Chinese and Indian claim lines along the Karakorum and Kunlun Mountain ranges. Reprinted from Central Intelligence Agency, Directorate of Inteligence, *The World Factbook, 1998* (Washington, DC: Printing and Photography Group, 1999), map 800911 (A06000) 9-88. Also available from http://www.cia.gov; Internet.

demarcate the boundary between India and China. Given its internal weakness and negative experiences with negotiating boundary treaties with foreign powers, China demurred, satisfied that the inaccessibility and harsh geography and climate would suffice to protect the undeclared border.

Consequently, the British Boundary Commission embarked on an effort to survey the region to better define the northeast boundary. Several expeditions went forth, drawing multiple variations of what the boundary should be. Commissioner Vans Agnew and his assistant Captain Alexander Cunningham proposed the most westerly boundary alignment, conforming to the general watershed of the Karakorum range. However, in 1865, a British survey officer, W. H. Johnson, delimited the border northeast of the Aksai Chin (up to the Kunlun Mountains), judging that despite the inhospitable nature of the terrain and weather, the border area was important because it lay astride trade routes linking Tibet and Xinjiang.[8]

British policy was to use China to prevent contact between the Russian and British empires. This was the most eastern border alignment of the eleven variations proposed and would be the basis of subsequent Indian claims to the Aksai Chin 93 years later. Analysis by Major General D. K. Palit in his book *War in the Himalaya* suggests that, being born in India, Johnson was inferior in status within the British Survey Department.[9] Consequently, he pursued his ambitions via the Maharaja of Kashmir, advancing claims to the 18,000 square kilometers of the Aksai Chin and up to the Kunlun

---

[8]Ibid., 14.

[9]Palit, 28.

mountains in an effort to secure favorable compensation. Kashmir maps would reflect this delimitation and again be used to substantiate later Indian territorial claims. However, British survey officers identified significant errors in his work and refused to officially recognize its delimitation. Palit observes Johnson's reward for promoting such a delimitation was his subsequent passover for promotion by the survey office, his resignation from the survey office and later employment by the Kashmiri Maharaja as the Governor of Leh.

During the next several decades, the British depicted the northern border of Kashmir differently at different times, according to the influence of various advocates and the degree of perceived threat from Russia.[10] In 1873, British maps still showed the boundary between India and China running along the natural geographic features of the Karakorum mountain range (southwest of the Aksai Chin), but alarm over Russian encroachments in Xinjiang to the north caused many to advocate moving the boundary further northeast to the Kunlun mountains, absorbing the Aksai Chin as a buffer between India and Russian expansion into Xinjiang. However, by 1885, Ney Elias, the British Joint Commissioner at Leh, determined that the natural watershed of the Karakorums was the only natural and defensible border between Kashmir and China and convinced the Foreign Office to maintain the Karakorum boundary.

In 1890, China reoccupied Shahdula and pushed south back to the Karakorums. China informed the British that it viewed the boundary between it and India as running along the Karakorums and the watershed between the Indus River and the Tarim Basin.

---

[10]Ibid., 32.

70

The British Foreign Office responded by sending a dispatch to the Secretary of State for India in Whitehall, which observed that "We are inclined to think that the wisest course would be to leave them in possession. . . . [I]t is evidently to our advantage that the tract of territory intervening between the Karakorum and the Kunlun mountains should be definitely held by a friendly power like China."[11] In 1893, the Chinese placed a boundary marker in the Karakorum Pass to demarcate this claim. This move was welcomed by the British as filling the void of the Aksai Chin and fulfilling Britain's desire to establish a buffer between India and growing Russian expansion to the South. "The Karakorum Pass thus became a fixed and mutually accepted point on the Sino-Indian border, but on both sides of the Pass, the alignment continued indefinite."[12] In 1891-92, Chinese survey officials explored the border region and delimited the Aksai Chin as lying within Chinese territory, contrary to Johnson's 1865 assertions. This issue was raised to the British who concurred, acknowledging that despite the Russian threat, such a forward position in difficult and inaccessible terrain was too difficult to support logistically and unnecessary as no hostile advance could be foreseen there for the same reasons. Therefore, from the British perspective, there was no advantage to securing territory (Aksai Chin) north of the Karakorum Mountain range.[13] India's failure to acknowledge this reality would exact a heavy price politically and militarily in 1962, yet current Indian views on the war still

---

[11]Ibid., 26.

[12]Maxwell, 17.

[13]Ibid., 19.

71

exhibit resentment at what they deem as British "ineptitude" and "acquiescence" in surrendering what they refer to as the Karakash valley (Aksai Chin).

In 1892, the Viceroy Lord Elgin proposed that the boundary run along the natural watershed of the Karakorum, specifically refuting the Johnson Line. Concurrently, General Ardagh, Director of Military Intelligence at the War Office, advocated the Johnson Line based solely on British strategic interest. Elgin's proposal succeeded and was incorporated into an official British governmental proposal to China to delimit the border, however the latter still refused to acknowledge any necessity to formerly delimit the border beyond local traditional convention.

In light of China's unwillingness to address the broader border issue, Britain established in 1893 the Durand Line, running 1,500 miles along the crest of the Afghan-Indian mountains. This action was taken with the express purpose of establishing a buffer between British interests and the Russian Empire. It was illogical in terms of local geography and ethnography.[14] Afghani acquiescence was given in context of its interests in containing Persia (also of British-Russian mutual interest). In 1899, The British proposed the MaCartney-Macdonald Line, giving China the Karakash Valley and almost all of the Aksai Chin and leaving India with the Lingzi Tang Salt Plains and all of the Changchenmo Valley and the Chip Chap River to the North. Beijing did not respond to this proposal and local Chinese made no objections: Henceforth the British accepted this

---

[14]Ibid., 9.

as the official boundary.[15] Unfortunately, this tacit boundary was never demarcated and few official maps were updated to reflect the change.

In 1912, after the fall of the Ching Dynasty, the British expected the Russians to annex Xinjiang. The Viceroy, Lord Harding, advocated pushing the Indian Border from the 1899 line to an earlier proposed line (Johnson-Ardagh Line) to preempt Russian annexation of Xinjiang. This proposal was rejected by the British Foreign Office, but was published on some Indian maps and would later become the basis of Indian claims to the Aksai Chin. World War I and the Russian revolution temporarily halted any further encroachments into Xinjiang. In 1927, the Governor of India determined that the northwest frontier with China and the boundary from Afghanistan to the Karakorum Pass ran along the crest of the Karakorum Range, rather than far to the north as prescribed by the Johnson-Ardagh Line.[16] For unknown reasons, this was not published on any Indian maps.

According to Neville Maxwell (Institute for Commonwealth Studies at Oxford University), "Britain had never attempted to exert authority on Aksai Chin, or to establish outposts in it, much less to set up posts or exercise authority up to a boundary on the Kunlun Range on the other side."[17] Britain did, however, vie with China for influence over Nepal, Sikkim, and Bhutan with the intent of seeking buffer states from China. Britain did establish a protectorate over Bhutan and was able to halt commercial

---

[15]Ibid., 18.

[16]Ibid., 23.

[17]Ibid., 24.

73

penetration, which was potentially destabilizing and provocative to the local tribesmen as well as the Russians and Chinese. However, Britain did have commercial interests in Lhasa, and accordingly sent an expedition to the Tibetan capital. This caused the Dalai Lama to flee to China and a regent was forced to sign an Anglo-Tibetan convention conceding British commercial and extraterritorial rights in Tibet. The Chinese government later ratified the agreement in the 1906 convention after negotiating a concession that the British would agree not to annex Tibet or interfere with Chinese administration over Tibet. In 1907, the British and Russians signed an agreement to keep out of Tibet, to negotiate with Tibet through China, and to respect Tibet's territorial integrity. By doing so, both had tacitly reinforced Chinese suzerainty over Tibet.

By 1910 China changed its policy regarding protectorates to forestall the further erosion of its control over territories. They dispatched an army to secure Tibet which would now become a full province of China. China began to extend its military presence in Tibet and to reduce both the British and the Dalai Lama's influence. The latter fled to India. This caused the British to view China as a threat to tea and coal rich Assam in northeast India. Consequently, they began to assert their administration in the Tawang Tract in the northeast frontier. In the aftermath of the 1911 revolution, Britain annexed the Tawang, despite recognizing it as Chinese. Simultaneously they sought to undermine China in Tibet. In 1913, they unsuccessfully attempted to get the Chinese to accept British administration in "outer Tibet," while recognizing Chinese suzerainty over all of Tibet. However, during the negotiations, the British under Henry McMahon (who assisted Durand in delimiting the border in 1893) secretly and illegally under the

74

provisions of the Anglo-Chinese convention of 1906, signed a bilateral agreement with Tibet demarcating the "McMahon Line" as the Tibet-Assam border.[18] This was contrary to instructions from London and annexed 2,000 square miles of Tibet, pushing the boundary from the strategically vulnerable foothills to the crest of the Himalayas. Later Indian accounts of the Simla Convention claim that Tibet was an equal participant at the conference and that Chinese representatives, albeit reluctantly, consented to the border arrangement in accordance with the McMahon Line, though they do acknowledge that it was never ratified by Beijing. General Palit, as do most Indian scholars, claims that the Simla Convention decided the Indian-Tibetan border with the tacit agreement of the Chinese, but failed to resolve the question of the Sino-Tibetan border.[19]

McMahon did state that the new boundary was not official and "should be open to modification should it be found desirable in light of more detailed knowledge acquired later."[20] Tibet ceded the territory in order to undermine Chinese authority and to gain the support of the British in achieving that objective. In all probability, China itself was unaware of the arrangement. According to Maxwell, the Simla Conference produced no agreement to which China was a party. Furthermore, Tibet, under the recognized suzerainty of China, was not sovereign and therefore had no treaty powers. This secret agreement was not known until 1937, at which time it was "forcefully repudiated" by both the Nationalist and the Communist Chinese as illegal.

---

[18]Ibid., 38.

[19]Palit, 41.

[20]Maxwell, 52.

Between 1914 and 1938 the British made no attempt to assert the provisions of

the secret treaty or to enforce the McMahon Line. Even Lhasa disregarded the McMahon

Line and refused to acknowledge British rights to Tawang, given the failure of the British

to secure Tibetan autonomy from China. The quid pro quo of the secret treaty was

unfulfilled. In the eyes of the Tibetans, the treaty was abrogated and therefore nullified.

However, by 1939, the Japanese invasion of China in 1937 caused Britain to unilaterally

claim the McMahon line as the official boundary. The British, while acknowledging that

racially and culturally the people were closer to Tibet then to Assam and that the line was

not a natural boundary, pushed out the Tibetan tax collectors and filled the vacuum which

had been previously allowed to persist.[21]

In 1947, the newly independent Government of India assumed control of the chain

of Himalayan protectorates from the British. India also encouraged Tibetan separatism.

When the Nationalist Chinese government fell in 1949, the Tibetans expelled the Chinese

mission in Lhasa and requested military aid from India. The Tibetans believed the

departure of the British offered an opportunity to recover territories ceded under the

Simla Convention and the secret treaty. Nevertheless, the Indians unilaterally continued

the 1939 British policy, claiming all territory south of the McMahon Line as Indian and

tacitly claiming territories encompassed in the unofficial and extreme Ardagh-Johnson

Line. The last act of the Nationalist Chinese ambassador in New Delhi was to remind the

Indian government that China did not recognize the McMahon Line and held the Simla

---

[21]Ibid., 50.

Convention invalid.[22] After defeating the Nationalist, the Communists immediately

began to regain influence in Tibet and in 1950, reoccupied it under the protest of India.

Nevertheless, despite these protestations, India recognized Chinese suzerainty over Tibet

and did not support Tibet's appeal for assistance to the United Nations.

The Indians did respond in 1951 by pushing into Tawang with the intent of

moving the de facto border from Sela to the McMahon Line: India's geostrategic

interests in maintaining a buffer were no different than that of the British. The Tibetans

protested without response and China's failure to protest was interpreted by the Indians as

an acquiescence of the McMahon Line. Likewise, Prime Minister Nehru unilaterally

adapted one of the eleven different British variations of the boundary in the Northwest

with the intent of preempting the issue. The Chinese demurral on the unilateral Indian

actions again reflected the Chinese belief that boundary negotiations are best left until

they can be conducted from a position of strength.[23] Yet, the Chinese did protest the

Indian encroachments as "not in conformity to the principles of non aggression and

friendly coexistence as codified in the Panch Sheel agreement."[24] India's reply was that

the territory was Indian and that China should not interfere with India's domestic affairs.

In September of 1951, China requested that India, Nepal, and China meet to

formalize their borders. India accepted, but no meeting ever took place. In 1952 a

meeting on India's "inherited" rights in Tibet (with respect to trade and the status of

---

[22]Ibid., 61.

[23]Ibid., 75.

[24]Ibid., 80.

Indian citizens) took place, but no discussion on the borders was broached. In 1954 trade negotiations at Lhasa culminated in the Sino-Indian "Panch Sheel" agreement wherein India renounced all of its rights and privileges in Tibet as inherited from the British. However the agreement continued to ignore the border issue.

According to Indian accounts, Nehru first raised the question of the western border with Mao by referring to Chinese maps which delimited the Chinese border as including what India refers to as the Assam Himalay. Allegedly, Mao responded by stating that the maps were old and that China had not gotten around to revising them yet.[25] Yet no discussion addressed the question of the boundary along the Ladkah and Aksai Chin. It was not until October of 1958, when an Indian patrol confirmed the existence of a Chinese road (began in 1956) through the natural trading route in the Aksai Chin linking Xinjiang with Tibet, that both governments made official claims along the boundary in the West. Yet neither government directly addressed the border issue with the other. Maxwell observes that: "The two governments were on the best of terms, each country had filled out into the no man's land of importance to itself, and all that was needed was an agreement to give binding diplomatic expression to what by all experiences was a mutually satisfactory status quo."[26] Indian's claim that the Chinese failed to do so in order to conceal the construction of the strategic road which had, in their

---

[25]Palit, 43.

[26]Maxwell, 85.

analysis, begun construction as early as 1951, immediately after Chinese reoccupation of Tibet.[27]

During a 1956 visit to India, Zhou Enlai addressed the McMahon Line in the East (see figure 2). Though accepting the boundary with Burma as an accomplished fact under treaty, Zhou pointed out that China would not accept the McMahon Line where there existed no treaty basis. Therefore, from the Chinese perspective, the basis for treaty delimitation could only be the status quo.[28] Nehru mistakenly understood from this meeting that no boundary disputes existed. By 18 October 1958, India claimed that the Chinese-built road in Aksai Chin was through part of the Ladakh region, which had been "part of India for centuries." At this time India also made inquires into the status of a missing patrol sent out earlier that year to verify the existence of the Aksai Chin road. The Chinese revealed that the patrol was detained and subsequently deported for "intruding into Chinese territory." While India characterized the Chinese activity in Aksai Chin as an attempt to advance territorial claims and demanded that the border be settled in accordance with India's unilateral boundary claims, China insisted on negotiating the boundaries before a final settlement. Nehru's position was that "there can be no question of these large parts of India being anything but India, and there is no dispute about them."[29] Zhou's position was that "the Sino-Indian boundary has never been formally delimited" and that "historically, no treaty of agreement on the Sino-Indian

---

[27]Palit, 43.

[28]Neville Maxwell, *India's China War* (New York: Doubleday and Company, 1972), 89.

[29]Ibid., 92-93.

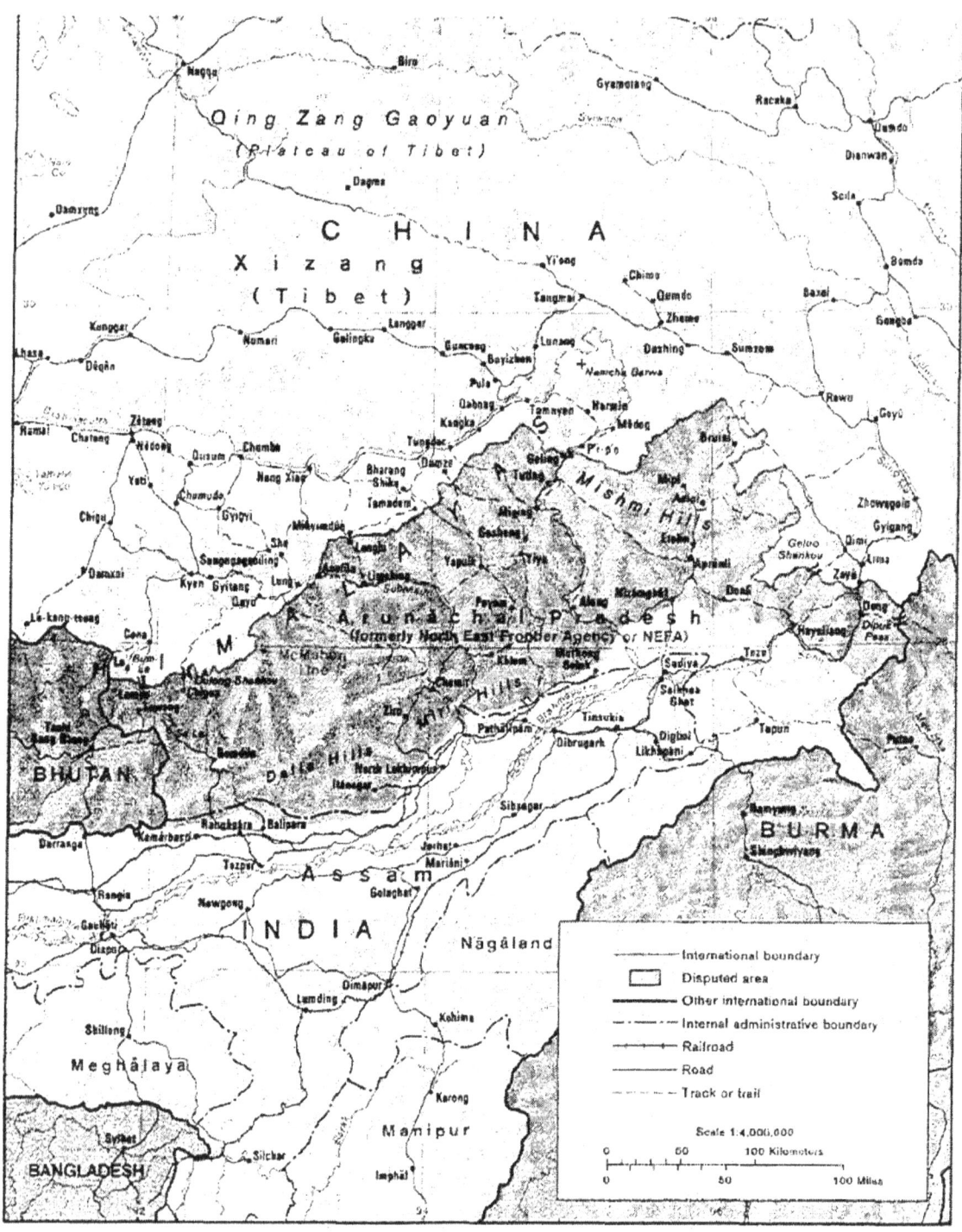

Figure 2. China India Border: Eastern Sector detailing McMahon Line, NEFA, and respective chinese and indian claim lines. Reprinted from Central Intelligence Agency, Directorate of Intelligence, *The World Factbook, 1998* (Washington, DC: Printing and Photography Group, 1999). Available from http://www.cia.gov; Internet.

80

boundary has ever been concluded between the Chinese central government and the Indian government."[30] He further pointed out that it would not be right to make changes without having surveyed the ground in consultation the neighbors concerned. As an interim solution, Zhou proposed that the two sides temporarily maintain the status quo. He further distinguished between the legality of the McMahon Line and the reality of current dispositions on the actual ground, signaling a compromise solution of Chinese willingness to accept the McMahon Line in the East for Indian acceptance of China's claims to the strategically vital Aksai Chin in the West. Yet India refused to consider quid pro quo or a negotiated compromise. Nehru incorrectly stated that India's boundary claims where legally derived from the Simla Convention and that the delimitation was based on natural geographic features and on tradition and custom. He further accepted China's proposal to maintain the status quo, but misinterpreted the status quo as the status quo ante, understanding that it meant a Chinese withdraw from the Aksai Chin to the Kunlun Mountains.[31]

On 25 August 1959, at Long Ju (east of the McMahon Line), Indian troops and Chinese troops were engaged in a brief firefight that both sides blamed on the other for starting, despite taking place on de facto Chinese occupied territory. India accused China of deliberate aggression in an attempt to implement its border claims by force. On September 1959, the situation was further exacerbated when the Khampa insurrection spread into Tibet. When the Dalai Lama proclaimed his support for the rebels and for

---

[30]Ibid., 93.

[31]Ibid., 97.

81

Tibetan independence, Chinese troops crushed the rebellion and forced the Dali Lama to flee to India. The result was an Indian backlash, sympathy for the Tibetan rebels, and a general condemnation of China. Furthermore, the Chinese became aware that the Indians were demarcating the boundary north of the McMahon Line itself in an attempt to reconcile the arbitrary boundary with natural features on the ground, but only in India's favor (i.e., further north).

During this period Nehru was under increasing pressure from the Indian parliament for both his domestic and foreign policy. In addressing the border issue to the parliament, Nehru played down the incidents and acknowledged a readiness to negotiate minor disputes on the McMahon Line but not the Aksai Chin, calling Chinese claims to "one half to the NEFA, one third of Assam, and one third of Bhutan, an affront to India."[32] His position hardened after Dr. S. Gopal, the Director of the Historical Division of the Ministry of External Affairs, stated that India had a stronger claim to Aksai Chin than did China, based on his erroneous reading of British maps[33] Thereafter, Nehru became implacable, referring to the border issue as one of national pride and self respect, and accusing China of acting out of pride, arrogance, and might in attempting to bully India.

On 8 September 1959, Zhou sent a letter to Nehru reaffirming his previous points: (1) that the boundary was never delimited; (2) that the 1842 treaty on the Western border and the Simla Conference on the Eastern border did not delimit the boundaries; (3) that

---

[32]Ibid., 117.

[33]Ibid.

82

China was not a participant to the 1842 treaty; (4) that the McMahon Line was not a product of the Simla Conference and had never been recognized by China; and (5) that the Aksai Chin was Chinese and had always been so in accordance with the customary boundary alignment.[34] Zhou further restated his desire for a settlement, fair to both sides, and considering historic background and existing actualities through friendly negotiations. He also requested that the trespassing Indian troops and administrative personnel be withdrawn.

Nehru erroneously perceived these statements as a veiled Chinese claim for all of the Indian NEFA north of Brahmaputra. Consequently, he directed that Indian patrols push deeper into the Aksai Chin, thereby threatening China's only land route between Xinjiang and Tibet. On 21 October, another action took place between Chinese frontier guardposts and Indian patrols at Konka Pass. Again, the incident took place on de facto Chinese territory and both sides placed blame on the other. Consequently, on 7 November, Zhou sent another message to Nehru proposing that both sides withdraw twenty kilometers from the McMahon Line in the east and also from the de facto line in Aksai Chin in the West. He also proposed a summit to negotiate the border dispute.[35] Nehru refused. In December, China made yet another offer, this time stating its willingness to accept the McMahon Line as the de facto border (surrendering China's legitimate claims south of that line) if India were to give up its (illegitimate) claims on the Aksai Chin.

---

[34]Ibid., 120.

[35]Ibid., 135.

Nehru counteroffered that each side withdraw to borders identified by the other

according to 1956 maps, in effect offering to give up only 50 square miles in the vicinity

of the McMahon Line while China would give up over 20,000 square miles of the Aksai

Chin in the west. This amounted to a unilateral Chinese withdraw, yet the Indian political

right in parliament condemned the offer as appeasement. Furthermore, Nehru rejected

the idea of a summit without first concluding a preliminary agreement. Zhou responded

that: (1) there was no need to treat the east and west sectors differently; (2) Nehru's

proposal was counter to the status quo (which he thought was agreed to by Nehru rather

than Nehru's concept of the status quo ante); (3) India' s proposal was unfair; and (4)

inquired whether India would apply the same approach to in the east where China had

legitimate claims well south of the McMahon Line (necessitating an Indian withdraw

from the NEFA).[36] India rejected the first three points and ignored the last.

Internationally, India had been perceived as the leader of the nonaligned

movement and as a peace mediator based on its neutral mediation efforts in conflicts in

Gaza, the Congo, and Korea. Consequently world opinion generally favored India and

blindly accepted India's propaganda with regard to the border dispute. The US attitude

toward India improved once it became apparent that Indian and Chinese relations were

deteriorating over the border issue. The Soviet Union initially assumed a neutral

position, which, given Soviet precedents, equated to tacit support for India. China

reacted angrily, reproaching the Soviets for "causing a virtual glee and jubilation among

the Indian

---

[36]Ibid., 143.

84

bourgeoisie, American and British imperialists, who use this to drive a wedge between China and the Soviet Union."[37]

The Soviet position was a result of additional factors which had already begun to fracture the Sino-Soviet alliance. Though the Soviets did support China's action against the Tibetan rebellion in March 1958, they feared that Mao's personal attacks against Nehru, referring to him as a double dealer, served to only reinforce the pro-Western elements in India, resulting in the disruption of Soviet peace overtures with the West and undermining the Indian Communist Party and other "progressive forces" within the country.[38] Additionally, Khruschev feared Mao's growing cult of personality, Mao's cavalier attitude toward the threat of a nuclear war, his ideological challenge to peaceful coexistence, and the counter productive nature of Chinese domestic policies like the Great Leap Forward. During a meeting with Zhou, Suslov, the leader of a Soviet delegation to China, expressed Khrushchev's position that:

> The Chinese comrades could neither correctly assess their own mistakes committed in their relations with India, nor the measures taken by the Central Committee of the Communist Party of the Soviet Union for the regulation of the Sino-Indian conflict--the Chinese leadership's assessment of the situation in India and the behavior of Nehru with regard to the conflict are undoubtedly erroneous and arbitrary.[39]

---

[37]James Hershberg, *The New East-Bloc Documents on the Sino-Indian Conflict, 1959 & 1962* (Woodrow Wilson International Center for Scholars; Cold War International History Project), 16; available from http://www.gwu.edu/nsarchive/cwihp.html; Internet; accessed 30 January 1999.

[38]Ibid.

[39]Ibid.

During the 2 October 1959 summit meeting in China, Khruschev detailed his rapprochement objectives with Eisenhower, emphasizing that "the incorrect actions of one country may hurt the international situation of the whole socialist camp. . . .[O]ne should keep in mind that imperialist propaganda directly link activity of Chinese comrades to the policy of the USSR and other socialist countries." Zhou responded, "We believe that if one carries out only the policy of unprincipled adjustment and concession to Nehru and the Indian government, not only would it not make them change their position for the better, but, on the contrary, in the situation of the growing offensive on their side, if China still does not rebuff them and denounce them, such a policy would only encourage their atrocity."[40] Clearly China would not subordinate its national interest to communist ideology or to the maintenance of an increasingly distasteful united front with the Soviet Union.

The Indians attempted to take advantage of this support but could not because the Soviets favored a negotiated settlement. Based on Soviet, and to a lesser degree international pressure, India reconsidered Zhou's summit invitation and dropped the precondition of a unilateral Chinese withdrawal. The result was more charges of appeasement from the right wing opposition in the Indian parliament, which Nehru by countered by asserting that there was a difference between agreeing to talk and negotiating a compromise. Nehru reiterated that there could be no negotiation over the Indian border claims. Domestically complicating the issue for India was a Supreme Court ruling on a previous border dispute between India and Pakistan which ruled that the

---

[40]Ibid.

adjustment of borders required ratification by two-thirds of the parliament and 51 percent

of the state legislatures (Berubari Amendment).[41]

Nehru continued to limit his options by using extreme rhetoric. He excited

national passions through exhortations to defend Indian honor and dignity which caused

popular opinion to demand resolute action to evict the Chinese from sacred Indian soil.

He publicly accused the Chinese of arrogance and aggression. By demanding

unconditional Chinese acquiescence to the Indian claim on the Aksai Chin without

negotiating, he made conflict inevitable. China attempted compromise by offering to

leave the boundary undelimited, with both sides observing the de facto line of control.

However, India countered by stating that this proposal was China's attempt to barter what

she held illegally against what she claimed unreasonably. Zhou also proposed that both

sides meet and examine all the historic evidence and prepare a report detailing each point

of agreement and disagreement. The only success achieved was a tacit agreement by both

sides suspend patrolling in the East.

Immediately after the summit, Zhou held a press conference, reiterating the

Chinese position and addressing "common points" between the two sides:

1. Boundary disputes between the two sides did exist

2. A line of actual control up to which each side exercises administrative
   jurisdiction did exist

3. In determining the boundary, certain geographical principles such as
   watersheds, river valleys, and mountain passes should be equally applicable to
   all sectors of the boundary

---

[41]Maxwell, 155.

87

4. A settlement of the boundary question between the two countries should take into account the national feelings of the two peoples towards the Himalayas and the Karakorum Mountains

5. Pending a settlement of the boundary questions between the two countries through discussions, both sides should keep to the line of control and not put forward territorial claims as preconditions, although individual adjustments may be made

6. To ensure tranquillity on the border, to facilitate the discussions, both sides should refrain from patrolling along the sectors of the boundary[42]

Nehru waited until Zhou departed before speaking with the press, stating that "there can be no question of barter in this matter." The following day in parliament, he again described the Chinese as aggressors, something he failed to do in direct meetings with Zhou. After the summit failure, the Chinese stance began to harden. At the same time, China signed bilateral treaties of friendship and boundary agreements with Bhutan and Nepal, usurping India's traditional role in governing their foreign affairs.

By calling the Chinese presence in Aksai Chin aggression, India was forced to act. The Indian opposition in parliament called for a direct confrontation, seeing not only the advantage of restoring Indian claims but also believing that war with the Chinese would unite and temper the Indian nation. To avoid both Indian acquiescence or a general war, Nehru established a Forward Policy of aggressive patrolling in the Ladakh to exercise an Indian presence within its claim lines. The objective was: (1) to block potential lines of further Chinese advance; (2) to establish an Indian presence in the Aksai Chin (giving the Indian territory to concede in a possible withdrawal agreement); and (3) to undermine

---

[42]Ibid., 167.

Chinese control of the disputed area by cutting off supply lines and forcing a Chinese withdrawal.[43]

Though the Indians were to patrol aggressively, they were not to directly attack Chinese positions. Inexplicably, Nehru irrationally assumed that the Chinese would not interfere with the Indian action, and did not take seriously the Chinese suggestion that India's aggressive patrolling in the Aksai Chin could be matched by the Chinese south of the McMahon Line. In explaining his strategy to the government, Nehru referred to the Forward Policy as a "police action" to push the Chinese out of Indian territory. He stated that India wanted to avoid war, but was ready to enforce India's rights if necessary. "There are some things no nation can tolerate: any attack on its honor, on its integrity, on the integrity of its territory, no nation tolerates, and it takes risks, even grave risks, to protect all that."[44]

Given the logistical difficulties and the challenging geography and climate, the Forward Policy was not implemented until August 1960. While senior Indian political and military officials dismissed the dangers of a possible Chinese reaction, professional army officers at the tactical level expressed grave concerns given the environment, the relative strength of the Chinese, and the relatively poor condition of the Indian army. Nevertheless, the policy began to make its impact in 1960 in minor border incidents which were followed by accusations and protestations by each side. That year China concluded a border treaty with Burma based on the status quo delimited by the British in

---

[43]Ibid., 178.

[44]Ibid., 183.

the nineteenth century. This arrangement demonstrated that "having repudiated all past boundary agreements with the British, the Chinese were in fact prepared to open negotiations on the basis of the very boundary lines the British proposed."[45]

The Indian government still refused to negotiate. In the interim, China pointed out that it had concluded border settlements with Burma, Pakistan, Bhutan, and Nepal (and would do so with Mongolia and Afghanistan in 1962). India was enraged by the Chinese agreement with Pakistan, which included a provisional delimitation of the China-Kashmir border. India protested that "there is no common border between China and Pakistan" and charged that the proposal to delimit "a non existent common border over territory that was legally Indian was a step in furtherance of aggressive aims that China has been pursuing toward India in recent years."[46]

By October-November of 1961, as Indian elections were approaching, the Nehru government was under pressure to demonstrate a strong policy. Increased Indian pressure on the western border resulted in more Chinese warnings: "The Chinese government deems it necessary to point out that it would be very erroneous and dangerous should the Indian government take the Chinese attitude of restraint and tolerance as an expression of weakness."[47] India continued to view Chinese warnings a bluff and replied to the Chinese protests and warnings by asserting that patrols were moving in Indian territory and that China's protests constituted an unwarranted interference in India's internal affairs.

---

[45]Ibid., 219.

[46]Ibid., 224.

[47]Ibid., 235.

Despite Nehru's claim that the use of force was never justified as a means of settling international disputes, in December, under political pressure to demonstrate strength and resolve in the wake of criticisms of its weak and appeasing foreign policy on China, India invaded the Portuguese colony of Goa, the last colony on the Indian continent. The government rallied public support with propaganda, referring to alleged Portuguese abuses, a build up in weapons which threatened India, and likely collaboration with Pakistan against India. The Indian armed forces provoked border incidents, and using them as a pretext, invaded and forced Portugal out of the colony. Maxwell stated this incident demonstrated Nehru's "susceptibility to excited political opinion and tendency to drift into courses of action that allowed no retreat, amorphous and subjective nature of decision making, and duality of attitude to the use of force."[48] In the context of the border dispute with China, Nehru stated, "The use of force is of course open to us and should be used by us according to suitability and opportunity." The Indian Home Minister, Lal Bahadur, also remarked that "if China will not vacate the areas occupied by her, India will have to repeat what she did in Goa."[49] Similar sentiments were expressed throughout the government as the euphoria of Goa overcame the reality that Portugal offered no resistance and that the Aksai Chin was not Goa and China was not Portugal.

Overconfidence reigned, encouraging more aggressive action against the Chinese in Aksai Chin. Forward patrols were now given orders to establish new posts in order to dominate existing Chinese posts in the area. The Chinese had already unilaterally

---

[48]Ibid., 239.

[49]Ibid., 240.

stopped patrolling within twenty kilometers of the de facto boundary and observed the McMahon line in the east, even if they still refused to recognize it. China continued to warn India of "grave consequences" if India continued its forward policy. By 1962, as India established new posts, China would respond by building more around each new Indian post. In April, China informed India that its border patrols (unilaterally suspended in 1959) would be resumed in the Aksai Chin, and warned that if the Indians continued their forward movement, China would resume patrolling along the entire frontier. China stated, "If such provocation continued, Chinese troops would be compelled to defend themselves and India would be responsible for the consequences."[50] In January, India began establishing new posts along the McMahon Line in the east. As long as the Indians remained south of the line, the Chinese did not react to these provocations. In May, the Chinese began conducting demonstrations of force against selected Indian posts in the Aksai Chin to demonstrate their vulnerability. (The Indian posts were widely dispersed and manned only at platoon level or less.) India characterized these demonstrations as "provocative Chinese advances into Indian territory," though the opposite was true. India then changed its rules of engagement for its forward posts from "fire only if fired upon" to "fire if the Chinese press dangerously close to your positions."[51]

Nehru reoffered his November 1958 proposal (a joint withdrawal to each others claim line), and ceded permission for the Chinese to use the Aksai Chin road for civilian traffic. India's message stated, "India does not want, and dislikes very much, a war with

---

[50]Ibid., 247.

[51]Ibid., 250.

92

China, but that is not within India's control."[52] The Chinese refused, noting that the

Indians were not prepared to apply the same protocol to legitimate Chinese claims south

of the McMahon Line, and stated that China "would never submit before any threat of

force."

On 12 July, as Indian forces pushed the Forward Policy deeper into Chinese

territory, another firefight erupted in the Aksai Chin. China again warned India:

> China, though prepared to exercise restraint and wishing to negotiate a settlement, cannot stand idle while its frontier guards are being encircled and annihilated by aggressors at this critical moment. The Chinese government demands that the Indian government order the Indian troops to stop attacking the (Chip Chap) post and withdraw from the area. If India should ignore the warning . . . and persist in its own way, India must bear full responsibility for all of the consequences.[53]

The Soviets, continued to apply pressure to India to negotiate. Consequently, on

26 July 1962, India offered to resume discussions, taking a less belligerent tone, but not

significantly altering its previous position. China accepted unexpectedly, but the Nehru

government ignored this positive response, probably fearing a domestic backlash. India

continued to demand a unilateral Chinese withdrawal. "To enter into negotiations of her

(China's) agreement to withdraw would have been to bring down on Nehru and the

government the opprobrious charges of appeasement and breech of faith from and

aroused and resentful political opinion in India."[54] Despite India's continued provocation

and refusal to negotiate, world opinion reminded firmly behind India, blindly believing

Indian propaganda and perceiving China as the aggressor in the dispute.

---

[52]Ibid., 251.

[53]Ibid., 264.

[54]Ibid., 258.

In August, the Indians began pressing north of the McMahon Line in the vicinity of Khinzemane, establishing a post and tenuously claiming that the area was Indian "by custom and treaty." The Chinese responded that Khinzemane was undoubtedly part of Chinese territory and that the Indian actions constituted serious encroachments upon Chinese sovereignty and territorial integrity. China then warned that that New Delhi would be responsible for the serious consequences if the Indian post was not withdrawn. China let the post stand until another one was established in the area vicinity Dohla (probably done inadvertently because of erroneous maps and a lack of clear communications between multiple echelons of Indian army command). This error caused the Chinese to respond with a large show of force. The Indian press decried the latest Chinese incursion and demanded action by the government. India, now aware of the true location of the post, irrationally decided not to withdraw but rather to continue expanding north to attempt to force the Chinese from the south face of the Thag La Ridge. China perceived India was actively extending its aggressive policy along the entire length of the Sino-Indian frontier, now unilaterally modifying the McMahon Line in the east as it had done so in the west in the Aksai Chin. To the Chinese, this represented a significant shift in India's policy which could not be ignored.

On 9 September, despite military objections to the tasks feasibility, India decided to forcibly evict the Chinese to the north side of the Thag La Ridge. The government believed that a hard and demonstrative blow to the Chinese beneath the Thag La Ridge would cause them to retreat and assume a more acquiescent attitude to future Indian moves elsewhere.[55] Indian forces made initial contact with the Chinese on 15 September, who attempted to negotiate a peaceful solution. Though no fighting took place, the Indians proceeded to establish supporting positions behind the Chinese in preparation for an attack.

On 20 September, another firefight occurred as a result of the new Indian Army rules of engagement, killing several Chinese soldiers. China responded by warning that:

> The situation in the area is extremely dangerous . . . and the flames of war may break out there. . . . Shooting and shelling are no child's play and he who plays with fire will eventually be consumed by fire. . . . [I]f the Indian side should insist on threatening by armed force the Chinese border defense forces . . . it must bear full responsibility for all of the consequences arising therefrom.[56]

The *Chinese People's Daily* reported that "the situation is most critical and the consequences will be serious. Let the Indian authorities not say that warning has not been served in advance."[57] On 23 September, a military dispatch was leaked to *The Times of India* detailing the political decision to force the Chinese from Thag La. Headlines in New Delhi papers boasted that a special task force was created to oust the Chinese and that the Indian army was "poised for an all out effort."[58]

On 10 October, as Indian forces were moving into final assault positions, the Chinese launched a spoiling attack, forcing the Indians back to their previous positions but not pursing them south of the Namka Chu River. This engagement marked the first

---

[55]Ibid., 333.

[56]Ibid., 268.

[57]Ibid., 341.

[58]Ibid., 350.

time the Chinese forcefully resisted an Indian move and directly attacked an Indian post.

India again decried Chinese aggression, ignoring the fact the Chinese attack preempted

their own and that the Indian forces were well north of the McMahon line. Soviet

Ambassador to India, I. A. Benediktov, discussed events with the provisional Charge

D'affairs of the Chinese embassy in India, E. Cheng-Chang. The latter stated that India

had gone too far for a normalization of relations to take place. According to Bendiktov's

personal diary, Cheng also claimed to have discussed the border clash with Menon, head

of the Indian Foreign Ministry's China Department. "During this conversation, Comrade

Cheng asked Menon to take a map of the eastern part of the border, published in India in

1960, and find on it the region in which the clashes are now occurring, orienting by

latitude and longitude the places indicated on the Indian notes. As a result it turned out

that this region, the latitude and longitude of which were indicated by the Indians

themselves, is located significantly north of the McMahon Line on Chinese territory."[59]

Despite the Indian setback, the Indian government's objective to forcibly eject the

Chinese remained. The government established a new date, 1 November, for the

completion of the task and reinforced the Army there with an additional Brigade to that

end.

Confronted with overt hostilities and an imminent Indian attack, China was forced

to act. Their alternatives consisted of the following: Either agree to withdraw from the

---

[59]Russian Foreign Ministry Documents on Soviet-Indian Relations and the Sino-Indian Border Conflict, 1962, *New East-bloc Documents on the Sino-Indian Conflict*, (Woodrow Wilson International Center for Scholars; Cold War International History Project), 6; available from http://www.gwu.edu/nsarchive/ cwihp.html; accessed 30 January 1999.

Aksai Chin to positions behind the Kunlun Mountains in accordance with Indian claim lines based on the Johnson-Agahda alignment (thereby surrendering to Indian military and political pressure the strategic road linking Xinjiang and Tibet and China's national pride) or resist India's encroachments with military action. China chose the latter.

Maxwell postulates several reasons for China's final decision to respond decisively to the Indian provocations:

1. The continuing loss of Chinese credibility in the face of Indian propaganda and force

2. The unacceptable costs of maintaining an indefinite readiness posture on the border, given the failures of the Great Leap Forward economic program

3. The opportunity to demonstrate real power to the Indians and the world

4. The adverse impact that Indian actions had on the Tibetan pacification

5. The implacability of India in refusing to even accept the status quo

6. The current vulnerability of the Indian army

7. The trend toward improved relations between India and the United States

8. Indian aggression in the east provided an opportunity to assert claims south of the McMahon LineMaxwell also states that a conflict with India would demonstrate the fallacy of the Indian presumption to equal or surpass China for the leadership of Asia and simultaneously demonstrate the fallacy of Moscow's fear of provoking the United States.

On 20 October 1962, China launched a major offensive against both the eastern and western sectors of the Indian frontier. China now adopted successful Indian propaganda tactics by accusing India of conducting a general offensive in both the east

97

and west (only true in the former). This claim was plausible given previous Indian leaks

to the press of impending military action against China and the government's optimistic

claims that India was prepared to force the Chinese out of India's claimed territory. On

24 October, the Chinese issued a statement recapitulating the course of the dispute and

acknowledging that the issue could not be settled by force. The statement further offered

to conduct peaceful negotiations and submitted the following proposals:

1. That both sides affirm that the dispute must be settled peacefully and agree to respect the line of actual control (as of November 1959) and withdraw their armed forces twenty kilometers behind that line.

2. If India agreed to the first point, Chinese forces would be withdrawn north of the McMahon Line.

3. That the Prime Ministers should meet again, in Beijing or New Delhi, to seek a friendly settlement.[60]

China accurately described its proposals as equal, mutually accommodatory, and

based on mutual respect,-not arbitrary or arrogant; however, India rejected the offer and

only hardened its position. By the twenty-fifth, China occupied the Tawang tract

unopposed.[61] India continued to subordinate military requirements to political

considerations, further compounding their fate on the battlefield. On the 29 October,

India publicly stated that it would accept the offer of US military aid and in doing so,

catalyzed the Chinese forces into decisive battle. On 19 November, Zhou informed the

Indian Charge D'affairs that:

---

[60]Maxwell, 398.

[61]Of additional interest, on 25 October the Soviets reversed their position because of the rapid development of the Cuban Missile Crisis, characterizing the McMahon Line as notorious, the result of British imperialism, and consequently illegal. The Soviets also accused India of being incited by imperialists and being the aggressors.

Beginning at midnight, the night of the 20th, the Chinese frontier guards will cease fire along the entire Sino-Indian border, and beginning on 1 December, the Chinese frontier guards will withdraw to positions 20 kilometers behind the line of actual control which existed between China and India on 7 November 1959. In the eastern sector, although Chinese frontier guards have so far been fighting on Chinese territory north of the traditional customary line (along the foothills of the pre-McMahon Line boundary), they were prepared to withdraw from their present positions to the north of the Line of actual control, that is north of the illegal McMahon Line, and to withdraw twenty kilometers back from that line. In the middle and Western sectors, the Chinese frontier guards will withdraw twenty kilometers from the line of actual control.[62]

Furthermore, Zhou stated that India was expected to do the same and that China reserved the right to strike back if India failed to do so. By 20 November, all Indian forces on the Chinese frontier had been soundly defeated and the Chinese had secured all territory within their original claim lines. India still refused to negotiate, but was incapable of changing the reality of the decisive Chinese victory. Despite public statements to the contrary, India's armed forces were directed not to break the cease-fire or provoke further Chinese action. Nehru sent a message to Zhou via Ceylon (Sri Lanka) that the Indian army would not attempt to retake its previous positions.[63]

China's decision to decisively respond to the Indian actions on the frontier was not motivated by its survival, which was never seriously threatened, unlike the circumstances which compelled its intervention in Korea. China's interest was to maintaining the strategic Aksai Chin road linking Xinjiang and Tibet and to protect China's territorial integrity. Without this route, China's lines of communication with Xinjiang would be forced through the Gobi desert and China would neither be able to

---

[62]Maxwell, 447.

[63]Ibid., 453.

exert effective control over the historically rebellious region nor contain Soviet

encroachments. Beyond this geostrategic interest, China now had the ability to protect its

territorial integrity and reverse the trends of the previous century. India's adoption of

"imperialist" boundary conventions and its attempt to assert its interests represented an

unacceptable throwback to the humiliating past and a challenge to China's self perceived

future as Asia's natural leader. It further raised the specter of establishing a precedent

which, if left unchecked, could be emulated by other neighbors, principally the Soviet

Union.

According to recently available records detailing a conversation between Zhou

and Mongolian leader J. Zendenbal which took place in Beijing on 26 December 1962,

Zhou offered the following rationale for the decision to respond with military force:

> The Indian side put us in an intolerable position. We were forced to take
> measures to defuse the situation. India began a new invasion and set off a
> conflict. We rebuffed them since it was such a serious situation. We have taken
> measures to defuse the situation. We have ceased fire and pulled our troops back.
> These are unilateral steps. . . . [T]he cause (of the conflict) is the aggressive
> policies of the ruling circles of the Indian government. Nehru is wavering and
> turning away from neutrality. India did indeed declare non alignment to
> aggressive blocs, but became ever more dependent on American dollars. . . . India
> is getting ever further on the side of reactionary imperialists.[64]

China's multiple attempts at negotiating a peaceful settlement and remarkable

restraint in the face of armed hostility against territory historically under Chinese

dominion demonstrate that China's interest lay not in territorial expansion, but in the

recognition of its legitimate territorial integrity and national interests by its neighbors.

---

[64]Cold War International History Project, *New East-bloc Documents on the Sino-Indian Conflict* (Woodrow Wilson International Center for Scholars; Cold War International History Project), 14; available from http://www.gwu.edu/nsarchive/cwihp.html; Internet; accessed 30 January 1999.

China possessed the military capability to unilaterally force the issue since 1954 but did not do so. It was only after repeated Indian encroachments and the deliberate use of force by India to secure the Aksai Chin that China exercised its military power and then only to secure its perceived legitimate claim lines. Though in an unchallenged position to exploit its tactical success, China instead withdrew to its historic boundaries.

Prime Minister Nehru's perception of the causes of the conflict was that Zhou, who had with Nehru championed the rise of the Non Aligned Movement only a few years earlier, opposed the current military policy against India, but that "leftist dogmatist sectarians within the Chinese leadership lead by Liu Shaoqi, supported it, not because of the border dispute but to strike a blow against the general phenomenon of neutrality in order to discredit Moscow's line of peaceful coexistence and competition with the West, and avoiding a general nuclear war."[65] Yet, India's irrational intransigence and bellicosity cannot be explained in any terms other than its own desire to rid itself of its colonial status and assert its newfound sovereignty and status as the leader of the nonaligned world. Ignorance may also have played a significant role, but it is the author's view that India deliberately chose to disregard the historical evidence and take advantage of the British fait accompli (clearly Britain and the United States were aware of the falsity of India's claim to the Aksai Chin, but chose to ignore it in context of the cold war).

As seen prior to intervention in Korea, China delivered clear warnings to India (beginning as early as April 1962) and did not attempt to deceive India of China's true interests or intentions. Again, India and the world chose to ignore those warnings and

---

[65]Ibid., 9.

101

failed to acknowledge China's legitimate security and territorial interests. Additionally, the world also ignored its initially peaceful overtures and labeled China the aggressor in the dispute. Consequently, China had no real alternatives, nothing to lose and everything to gain, by its action against India. In taking the course of a limited offensive to preserve its territorial integrity, China also demonstrated its military capability, resolve, and diplomatic credibility.

CHAPTER 5

VIETNAM

> We have no eternal allies, and we have no perpetual enemies. Our
> interests are eternal and perpetual, and those interests it is our duty
> to follow.[1]

Lord Palmerston

On 17 February 1979, after several years of tensions and deteriorating relations,

China invaded across the Sino-Vietnamese border with over 330,000 ground troops in a

costly limited struggle which lasted only sixteen days. This chapter seeks to examine the

events leading up to the crisis and the key factors involved in China's decision to conduct

a limited punitive war against its erstwhile ally in Asia. It will also examine a brief

history of the relationships in the region, the relative interests of each of the players

(China, Vietnam, and the Soviet Union), the impact of the first and second Indochinese

wars, the relationship with the Soviet Union, border disputes, Vietnam's policy on ethnic

Chinese, and finally, the dénouement, the issue of Kampuchea.

Historically, China has maintained a traditionally dominant relationship over

Vietnam. Relationships were characterized by Vietnam's payment of token tribute to

China and the tacit recognition by China of Vietnam's de facto autonomy. By the end of

World War Two, both China and Vietnam were confronted by the declining remnants of

the imperial era of the previous century and sought the same objectives: national

---

[1]Alan Plamer and Veronica Palmer, *Quotations from History* (Sussex: Harvester Press, 1976),
175.

security, reunification, cessation of foreign intervention, economic development, and the assertion of national power and influence.[2]

During the first Indochinese war against France, from 1950 to 1954, and the second Indochinese war with the United States from 1964 to 1975, China provided military and economic assistance to Vietnam. China did not deem it necessary to intervene directly in the conflict because its security was not at stake and because of its own economic and internal political challenges, particularly during the aftermath of the Korean war and the turbulence of the Cultural Revolution.

In 1950, China offered massive aid to the communist Vietminh in Indochina to fight the French colonialists. This assistance to the Vietminh, coupled with the employment of Chinese military advisors, resulted in the success of a fall offensive during that year, ultimately establishing the conditions necessary for the final collapse of the French during the Dien Bien Phu campaign (December 1953 to May 1954). The capture of Dien Bien Phu occurred one day prior to the opening of the Geneva Conference on Indochina. The participants included Britain, the Soviet Union (both co-chairmen), China, the United States, the Vietminh, South Vietnam, Laos, and Cambodia. The initial negotiations were focused on establishing a cease-fire, which was predicated upon a withdrawal of Vietminh forces from Laos and Kampuchea; however, disagreements between the Pathet Lao revolutionary government and the Khmer Rouge faction with the Vietminh prevented any coherent negotiation with the French. Zhou Enlai persuaded the Vietminh to withdraw from Laos and Cambodia and offered to

---

[2]King C. Chen, *China's War with Vietnam* (Stanford: Hoover Institution Press, 1986), 1.

recognize the two Royal governments under the condition that no American bases would be built in the two kingdoms.[3] Zhou met with the French Premier Pierre Mendes at Bern, Switzerland, where they both agreed on an armistice governing the three Indochinese states, a political settlement calling for the recognition of Laos and Cambodia, and national elections to determine the leadership of a unified Vietnam.

The settlement of the temporary demarcation of Vietnam along the 17th parallel was negotiated during the period of 10 to 21 July 1954, with final unification to take place as determined by national elections two years later. During this period, both sides agreed on the composition of the International Commission for Supervision and Control (Poland, Canada, and India) and banned any military alliances with the Indochinese states. Given the subsequent blocking of national elections by South Vietnam and the United States in 1958, North Vietnam would later accuse China of betraying the Indochinese revolution by preventing the Vietminh from liberating all of Indochina and of colluding with the French imperialist to keep Indochina separated and weak.

During the second Indochinese war China continued to provide military support to North Vietnam, including a squadron of MIG-15 and MIG-17 aircraft and sanctuary airfields in Yunnan and Guangxi. The US decision to bomb Hanoi in 1965 resulted in the Soviet Union changing its previous policy of rapprochement with the US and non-involvement in Indochina. Moscow proposed a Sino-Soviet united front approach in opposing the United States in Vietnam. Specifically, Moscow requested: (1) transit routes through China for Soviet weapons; (2) Soviet use of airfields in Yunnan and the

---

[3]Ibid., 13.

right to station 500 Soviet support personnel; (3) Soviet air corridors over China; (4)

permission for 4,000 Soviet military personnel to transit China enroute to Vietnam; and

(5) trilateral talks between the Soviet Union, China, and Vietnam.[4] Pham Van Dong of

North Vietnam supported the proposal but China refused, agreeing only to the transit of

Soviet supplies through China to North Vietnam. Mao's decision was made in the

context of competition with the Soviets for the leadership of the communist bloc as well

as the deterioration of relations between the two nations since the Sino-Indian conflict.

Chinese policy regarding the war was to increase military and economic aid to offset

Soviet influence while at the same time encouraging North Vietnam to pursue a strategy

of self-reliance and people's war against the US. China's primary interest was in

preventing another Sino-American war. China would not directly intervene in the

conflict unless the US introduced the ground war into North Vietnam (posing a threat to

Chinese security by threatening a neighboring buffer state), or China itself was attacked.

Chinese policy on the growing crisis with Vietnam was formulated during the

turbulence of the cultural revolution, which began in November 1965, and the growing

animosity in its relationship with the Soviet Union. Given this turbulence, Mao decided

to limit aid to Vietnam and frame foreign policy decisions in the context of the overriding

objective of impeding growing Soviet influence in Asia. Any conflict in Vietnam

involving the US and China would benefit only the Soviets. Therefore, it was to be

avoided unless China's own security interests were placed directly at risk.

---

[4]Ibid., 17.

By 1967 Hanoi had shifted its policy away from deference to Beijing and toward an independent strategy in the war against the US. After the 1968 Tet Offensive, President Johnson offered to hold talks with the North Vietnamese, which was accepted by the latter without consulting the Chinese. China, annoyed over Vietnam's independent course, carried a news blackout of the Paris Peace talks for seven months. In the meantime, the Soviet Union invaded Czechlosovakia. China condemned the action as "socialist imperialism," further straining the relations between the two communist giants. Vietnam, by this time succumbing to the influence of its dependence on Soviet military aid, supported the Soviet decision. In March 1969, Sino-Soviet tensions manifested themselves in the border clash on the Ussuri River. Given Soviet armed hostility on China's northern border and in Czechoslovakia and the deteriorating position of the United States in Vietnam, Mao now perceived the Soviets as the principal threat to China and its interests in South East Asia.

Relations with Vietnam improved briefly in September 1969 with the death of Ho Chi Minh. Zhou made a visit to Hanoi to pay his respects, and this visit was reciprocated by Pham Van Dong shortly thereafter. The death of the politically astute Ho Chi Minh, who was able to effectively play the Soviets and the Chinese off of one another to Vietnam's benefit, offered the Soviets an opportunity to expand their influence in Asia. Soviet interest in Indochina was a result of its competition for regional and international influence with both China and the United States. The Soviet goals in Asia were: (1) to replace the United States as the premier power in Asia, (2) to counter Chinese influence, (3) to support communism, (4) to obtain vital warm water ports, and (5) to exert its influence by making the region dependent upon Soviet military and economic aid. The Soviets promoted the pro-Soviet Le Duan as the successor to Ho by offering massive military and economic aid.

Additionally, the Soviets proposed a collective security arrangement for Asia, offering aid and political agreements to communist and noncommunist states alike.[5] China denounced the Soviet initiative as an attempt to encircle China. Despite the political ascendance of the pro-Soviet Le Duan over the neutral pragmatist Pham Van Dong, Vietnam continued to resist Soviet overtures to sign a treaty of friendship and cooperation and denied Soviet requests to use newly acquired bases in Vietnam. This was done to avoid compromising its pivotal position within the Sino-Soviet-Vietnamese triangle. Vietnam's policy with both countries was to take advantage of their competition and to ultimately gain greater independence from both powerful neighbors after the war. Consequently, Vietnam remained silent on the Soviet proposal for a Soviet-Asian collective security alliance.

The March 1970 coup in Kampuchea, led by the US-backed Lon Nol, and the joint US-South Vietnamese invasion of Laos in February 1971, resulted in North Vietnam inviting Zhou to Hanoi to discuss the escalation of the war. Both countries issued a joint communiqué stating that if the US expanded the war in Indochina, China was determined to take all necessary measures to support the Indochinese people and "not flinch even from the greatest national sacrifices."[6] Nevertheless, given Hanoi's political shift toward

[5]Ibid.

[6]Ibid.,19.

108

the Soviet Union and China's fear of Soviet expansionism in Asia, China pursued

improved relations with the US, secretly inviting Henry Kissinger to Beijing in July 1971

and ultimately President Nixon in 1972. The Vietnamese regarded these events as the

second betrayal of Indochina by the Chinese. Additionally, in January of 1973, as a

direct result of US bombing to pressure North Vietnam, Hanoi signed the Paris Peace

Agreement, which preempted an immediate North Vietnamese victory and the

establishment of an Indochinese federation. China publicly praised the settlement, further

reinforcing Vietnamese mistrust of China. Exacerbating this mistrust was China's seizure

of several Paracel Islands, claimed by both North and South Vietnam.

Further heightening Hanoi's suspicions was China's recommendation that

Vietnam pursue a gradual approach to achieving its victory in reunifying all of the

country. Given the political developments within the US (Watergate, passage of the War

Powers Act, the Helsinki Accord with the Soviets, and the country's desire to extract

itself from Indochina), Hanoi decided to aggressively exploit South Vietnam's weak

position, resuming offensive operations in 1974. China, concerned over these

developments, as well as Soviet adventurism in Angola and Mozambique, invited

Kissinger to Beijing from 10-13 November 1973 to discuss China's concerns and to

preempt any potential US-USSR collusion. At the end of the meeting, both parties issued

a joint declaration opposing global hegemony.

Concurrently, China sought rapprochement with Thailand, offering to cease

aiding the Thai communist party and highlighting the threat posed by a Soviet backed

Vietnam. Vietnam also attempted to improve relations with Thailand; however, it

109

refused to cease providing aid to the CPT (Communist Party of Thailand) and thereby

undermined its efforts. China viewed ASEAN (Association of Southeast Asian Nations)

as an obstacle to Soviet expansion and aggressively established relations with those states

sharing a common interest in containing both Vietnamese and Soviet influence in the

region. On 1 July 1975, China and Thailand established diplomatic relations and signed a

joint communiqué which included an anti hegemony clause directed against Vietnam and

the Soviet Union. China also attempted to foster closer relations between Thailand and

Kampuchea. On 31 October 1975, Thailand and Kampuchea established diplomatic

relations and signed a similar joint communiqué including a like anti hegemony clause.

With the 1973 peace settlement and subsequent withdraw of US forces from

Vietnam, the PGNU government of Laos (Vientiane Coalition) was established on 5

April 1974. Yet, 28,000-40,000 Peoples Army of Vietnam troops remained in the

country along the Ho Chi Minh trail to continue to provide logistical support to the

Communist Vietcong still fighting a guerrilla war in South Vietnam.[7] Economic and

technical aid agreements enabled both Vietnam and China to maintain a significant

military presence in Laos even after the political settlement deadline for the withdrawal

of all foreign troops expired. China was equally determined to maintain its influence by

providing political and economic support to the Vientiane Coalition to offset aid given by

the Vietnamese. To counter Soviet airlift support to the Pathet Lao, China provided like

support in an attempt to limit growing Soviet influence in Laos as well. Despite these

efforts, China could not compete politically or logistically with Vietnam in the quest for

---

[7]Ibid., 123.

influence in Laos. By the end of March 1975, the Hanoi backed Pathet Lao moved

against the Vientiane government forces and established a regime under the influence of

North Vietnam. Consequently, China was determined to take any measures necessary to

prevent the expansion of Vietnamese and Soviet influence in Kampuchea.[8]

The specter of an imminent victory in South Vietnam and Laos emboldened North

Vietnam to expand its political and military pressure in Kampuchea to realize its ambition

to create an Indochinese Federation under Vietnam's leadership. Despite its distrust of

Saloth Sar, the leader of the communist National United Front of Kampuchea (NUFK),

Vietnam provided military support in the ongoing battle with the US supported

republican forces under Lon Nol. China provided additional support to ensure the

viability of an independent Kampuchea capable of resisting DRV influence. In March of

1974, the NUFK requested support from North Vietnam, China, and North Korea for its

final offensive to secure Phnom Penh. Hanoi offered support to NUFK by pledging

respect for Kampuchean independence, territorial integrity, and neutrality and by signing

an aid agreement in October. The Chinese provided substantial aid, motivated by its

desire to secure influence and to see the liberation of Phnom Penh prior to the liberation

of Saigon by the North Vietnam and the Provisional Revolutionary Government. Despite

the growing competition and divergence of interests, the Vietnamese remained dependent

upon Chinese aid to complete its final offensive in the South. China leveraged its

position by making such aid contingent upon Vietnamese cooperation in aiding the

NUFK.

---

[8]Ibid., 124-125.

By November 1974, China had successfully pressured the US to abandon its support for Lon Nol. With victory imminent, the NUFK Second National Congress proclaimed that Kampuchea would not tolerate any military bases of aggression on its soil and would not be a satellite of any foreign nation (an implicit reference to Vietnamese troops in Kampuchea). It further rejected North Vietnam's implication that wartime aid had entitled it to a special position with respect to Kampuchea.[9] Nevertheless, during the final NUFK offensive against Phnom Penh, North Vietnam contributed two divisions in an attempt to secure its influence in the new regime. The NUFK took Phnom Penh two weeks prior to the North Vietnamese liberation of Saigon. The Chinese provided significant support to the NUFK effort, in contrast to its lack of support to the North Vietnamese effort to take Saigon, principally supplied by the Soviet Union. Consequently, both China and the Soviet Union had established their respective spheres of influence in Indochina.

The new NUFK government, concerned over historic border disputes with Vietnam and the maintenance of its national identity, was suspicious of both Vietnamese and Soviet intentions. Consequently, it emphasized the importance of mutual assistance within the principles of independence, self-reliance, and respect for each other's sovereignty. In contrast, Hanoi emphasized the importance of Indochinese strategic unity and the implicit dominance of the Vietnamese revolution in Indochina.[10] These disparate objectives quickly began to manifest themselves in border clashes and in a dispute over

---

[9]Ibid., 127.

[10]Ibid.

112

the ownership of the Phn Quoc and Puolo Wat Islands. By June 1975, Pol Pot and Ieng Sary had consolidated leadership over the NUFK and proposed to Vietnam a Treaty of Friendship and Nonaggression. Vietnam rejected the offer, insisting on a treaty of Friendship and Cooperation.

On 30 April 1975, the South Vietnam regime fell, and with it the impetus for Vietnamese and Chinese cooperation. Consequently, China ended its aid program to North Vietnam. In 1976, at the request of the Thai government, the United States withdrew the remainder of its troops from Thailand, causing concern to China that the resulting power vacuum in Asia would be filled by the Soviets and their Vietnamese surrogate. China perceived itself vulnerable to the threat of encirclement by the specter of Soviet power projection bases in Vietnam and Laos. China became trapped in the classic security dilemma: any support it provided to North Vietnam would only strengthen its regional antagonist, yet failing to do so would result in the self-fulfilling prophecy of pushing the Vietnamese further under the influence of the Soviets. Likewise, China wished to avoid an expanded conflict between Vietnam and Kampuchea, fearing that an exacerbation of the deteriorating Sino-Vietnamese relations would provide the Soviets a pretext for direct intervention in such a conflict. At the same time, Vietnam was becoming increasingly concerned over the specter of a Chinese-backed Kampuchea.

Both the Chinese and Vietnamese increasingly sought their own security by taking actions which unintentionally threatened the perceived security of the other.[11] The Chinese tactic of obstructing a strong Indochinese federation at the Paris Peace

---

[11]Ibid., 72.

negotiations and its occupation of the Paracel Islands solidified the pro-Soviet tilt within the Vietnamese leadership, as well as in Laos, which mirrored Vietnamese foreign policy. Kampuchea, fearing Vietnamese pressure on the border and the latter's attempts to assimilate Kampuchea into an Indochinese federation, began to ally itself more closely with China.

During this period, China was undergoing an internal struggle between the radical hard-liners, who wanted to aggressively oppose both the United States and the Soviet Union, and the moderates under Deng, who advocated balancing the two superpowers against one another.[12] The Paracel crisis of January 1974 reflected the growing influence of nationalistic radicals, and heralded the Vietnamese shift from a policy of balance to a pro-Soviet tilt. During the Paris peace accords, the Vietnamese astutely played their position within the Sino-Soviet-Vietnamese triangle. Vietnam had resisted Soviet attempts to sign a treaty of friendship and denied Soviet requests for use of bases, to prevent compromising its still useful relationship with China.

On 26 October 1974, the Soviets agreed to provide additional aid to Vietnam for 1975, and took the unprecedented step of promising to coordinate the Soviet five year plan with the Vietnamese five year plan. This aid, coupled with Vietnam's desire to accelerate reunification given the growing frequency and intensity of political and territorial disputes with China, enabled North Vietnam to conduct its final offensive in the south and achieve victory in April 1975. With its immediate objective secured, Hanoi promptly blamed China for prolonging the war, failing to deter US intervention,

---

[12]Ibid., 117.

114

undermining the Soviet proposal for united action, opposing Vietnamese negotiations with the United States, preventing the complete liberation of Vietnam at Geneva in 1954. China responded by accusing Vietnam of being ungrateful and of betraying Sino-Vietnamese friendship.

Nevertheless, desperate for postwar reconstruction funds, Vietnam approached both China and the Soviet Union for annual aid as well as support for the upcoming five year plan. Displaying its dissatisfaction with Vietnam's growing relationship with the Soviets, China granted only $200 million in aid for 1976, providing nothing for the five year plan. In contrast, the Soviets provided $500 million for 1976 and $3 billion for the five year plan.[13] While denying Vietnam's aid request, China simultaneously provided Kampuchea the equivalent of a $1 billion interest free loan for five years, plus an additional $20 million to cover Kampuchea's foreign debt.[14] Vietnam accused China of reneging on its aid commitments and of using aid as a tool to influence Vietnamese policy.

In 1976, the government of Democratic Kampuchea reorganized itself to reconcile opposing elements of Khmer communists and intellectuals. This liberalization was briefly reflected in a new non alignment in its foreign policy. Pol Pot was the Prime Minister and third in power, after Khiu Samphan (Head of the State Presidium), and Nuon Chea (Chairman of the National Assembly Standing Committee). However, during that year a series of policy and agricultural failures, coupled with increasing resistance to

---

[13]Ibid., 24.

[14]Anne Gilks, *The Breakdown of the Sino-Vietnamese Alliance, 1970-1979* (Berkeley: Institute of East Asian Studies, University of California, 1992), 143.

the draconian Khmer rule, enabled Pol Pot to purge his rivals and institute a genocidal program aimed at eliminating intellectuals, bourgeoisie, and alleged subversive agents within the Vietnamese wing of the ICP (Indochinese Communist Party). Not only were Vietnamese cadres eliminated, but also the history of the ICP itself. All recognition of the organization's formative role and of parentage of the KCP (Kampuchean Communist Party) was disavowed. Ultimately this resulted in creating a self-fulfilling prophesy, as purged classes fled to Vietnam and provided the nucleus of Khmer opposition to Pol Pot. Kampuchean nationalism (and personal survival) became increasingly tied to anti-Vietnamese rhetoric and policy. In January and February of 1977, the Kampuchean Central Committee Secretariat halted all participation in Vietnamese border liaison committees and adopted a program to confront Vietnam politically, diplomatically, and militarily.[15] Aided by the support of the radical elements within the Chinese government (as well as modern Chinese weapons), Kampuchea began to apply pressure on its border with Vietnam.

Alarmed by what it perceived as a deliberate Chinese policy of expansion on both its northern border with China and its southern border with Kampuchea, Vietnam purged all remaining pro-Chinese elements and abandoned any further attempt to balance itself between China and the Soviet Union. Vietnam moved aggressively to establish an Indochinese federation. On 5 February 1977, it proposed an immediate cessation of border hostilities, including the creation of a ten-kilometer demilitarized zone on the border, a nonaggression treaty, and a border treaty guaranteed by international

---

[15]Ibid., 173.

116

supervision. This was rejected by Kampuchea because it required recognition of the current border, viewed by Kampuchea as unfair. Kampuchea also rejected the treaty's implicit acquiescence to a special relationship with Vietnam.[16] As a precondition to any negotiations, Kampuchea demand that Vietnam first end its aggression and subversion in Kampuchea and abandon its pursuit of an Indochinese federation.[17]

As Soviet influence in Vietnam grew, China continued to assail Soviet and Vietnamese intentions. In early 1977, General Vo Nguyen Giap, visiting Beijing on his way back from Moscow, countered Chinese accusations of hegemony by stating that Vietnam had routed US imperialism without the need to oppose Soviet revisionism. The Chinese media responded by denouncing Vietnam as a running dog of Soviet revisionists. On 21 February 1977, Vietnam publicly accused "international reactionaries" (code word for China) of instigating Kampuchean aggression on the Vietnamese border. Accelerating the deterioration of relations was Vietnam's decision to forcibly expel ethnic Chinese from its northern border to eliminate a perceived security risk in the context of growing tensions.

By this time, the Soviets had 2,000 to 3,000 advisors in Vietnam. That figure would increase to 5,000 to 8,000 by 1979.[18] Of greater significance to the Chinese was the Soviet naval presence at Haiphong and Cam Ranh Bay. Beijing viewed this activity as a demonstration of Soviet imperialism and collusion in Vietnam's ambition of creating

---

[16]Ibid., 189.

[17]Ibid., 201.

[18]Chen, 25.

117

an Indochinese federation. Despite these developments, China attempted to control the

Kampuchean-Vietnamese conflict to preserve its tenuous relationship with Vietnam.

During the Fifth National People's Conference held on 26 February 1977, Hua Guofeng

reiterated that "socialist countries should resolve differences peacefully through friendly

consultation," without responding to the Vietnamese charge of Chinese provocation of

the Kampuchean-Vietnamese border conflict. At this time, China had not publicly linked

Vietnamese policy with Soviet hegemonism. However, Hua did issue a veiled warning:

> No country should seek hegemony in any region or impose its will on others.
> Whether a country treats others on an equal footing or seeks hegemony is a major
> criterion by which to tell whether or not it is . . . a genuine or sham socialist
> country. . . . We should get rid of great nation chauvinism, resolutely, thoroughly,
> wholly, and completely. . . . We will not attack unless we are attacked. If we are
> attacked we will certainly counter attack.[19]

On 27 September 1977, Chinese Foreign Minister Chiao Guanhua accused the

Soviets of filling the power vacuum in Indochina after they deployed MIG 21 fighters to

Laos. He warned Asian countries "not to let the tiger in the back door while repulsing the

wolf through the front gate."[20] On 20 November 1977, Le Duan visited Beijing, most

likely to discuss with Hua Guofeng the issue of Vietnam's continuing desire to establish

political dominance over Kampuchea. No mutually accommodating settlement was

reached. One month later, as a result of continuing Vietnamese pressure, Kampuchea

severed diplomatic relations with Vietnam.

---

[19]Gilks, 191.

[20]Ibid., 129.

At the Bandung Conference in 1954, Zhou assured Prince Norodom Sihanouk that

China would always support Kampuchea's independence and neutrality.[21] By 1956

Kampuchea had obtained $22 million in economic aid from China and established

diplomatic relations. In 1958 both countries signed a Friendship and Nonaggression Pact.

China's interest in Kampuchea was in preventing it from falling under Vietnamese

domination as part of an Indochinese federation. When Prince Sihanouk requested the

departure of the US mission to Kampuchea in 1963 as a result of US involvement in the

overthrow of Ngo Dinh Diem, China issued a statement supporting the prince and

pledging support against a possible armed intervention by the United States. After Lon

Nol's successful coup in March 1970, the Chinese sponsored an Indochina conference in

Guangzhou to determine a common course of action in response to the coup and the US

expansion of the war into Laos. The participants included Prince Sihanouk, leaders of the

Khmer Rouge, North Vietnam, and the Pathet Lao. China offered free weapons and

transport to the Khmer Rouge guerrillas fighting the Lon Nol regime. China's interest

was to maintain the independence and neutrality of Kampuchea from both the United

States and Vietnam.

In August of 1975, a delegation from the new Democratic Kampuchea, led by

Deputy Prime Minister Khieu Samphan, was invited to Beijing to conclude an agreement

for Chinese economic and technical assistance to Kampuchea and a pledge to "unite

against hegemonism," a reference to the growing Vietnamese pressure to join an

Indochinese Federation. Sihanouk, in exile in China since his defeat by Lon Nol, was

---

[21]Chen, 29.

invited back to Phnom Penh and returned to a hero's welcome in September 1975. During the ceremonies, the Defense Minister Son Sen stated that Kampuchea would "take draconian measures aimed at eliminating the North Vietnamese and Vietcong presence in Kampuchea once and for all."[22]

Within a short period of time, once the extremist and brutal nature of the Khmer Rouge regime under the new leadership of Pol Pot became evident, both Sihanouk and the Chinese became alarmed at political and social developments in Kampuchea. Zhou advised Khieu Samphan to adopt the Chinese experience in gradually transforming the country into a socialist state over the course of several years. This advise was ignored, resulting in the complete economic and social disintegration of Kampuchea. Likewise, the popular moderate Prince Sihanouk was suppressed and placed under virtual house arrest by the Khmer Rouge.

On July 1977, Kampuchean Defense Minister Son Sen visited Beijing. Deng severely criticized Kampuchea for its radical purge of Vietnamese cadres which raised the threat of an internal revolt and warned that China would not save Kampuchea unless it abandoned its sectarian policies and united all of the people. To that end he repeatedly suggested that the Khmer Rouge rehabilitate Prince Sihanouk and make him part of a coalition government. Deng also stated that in view of China's long-standing principles, as well as diplomatic an political reasons, China would not rescue Kampuchea in the event of an invasion by Vietnam.[23]

---

[22]Ibid., 31-32.

[23]Ibid., 207.

In July 1977, Laos agreed to a twenty-five-year Treaty of Friendship and Cooperation with Vietnam, along with an aid package, a border agreement, and a Joint Declaration. This agreement was the model for a similar arrangement Vietnam wished to apply to Kampuchea. Vietnam's previous negotiations with Kampuchea yielded no results other than accusations and border disputes. Kampuchea continued to insist on a treaty of friendship and nonagression, rather than cooperation. Vietnam refused, recognizing that such an agreement would by implication make Kampuchea independent and equal to Vietnam.

In 1978, after several years of repeated requests by the Khmer Rouge and international political pressure, Vietnam consented to remove its forces from Kampuchea. Vietnam resented the Kampuchean request, asserting that Kampuchea was liberated with the help of Vietnam and should therefore be treated as a "big brother." Vietnam was also angered by the ongoing purge by the Khmer Rouge of over 4,000 Vietnamese trained forces. Additionally, Pol Pot refused to agree to the Vietnamese concept of an Indochinese Federation (as acquiesced to by the Laotians) and continued to pursue closer ties with China.

Vietnam's desired relationship with the other Indochinese states was articulated during the Fourth Congress of the Vietnamese Workers Party in December of 1976: "to enhance military solidarity, mutual trust, and long term cooperation and mutual assistance in all fields between our country and fraternal Laos and Kampuchea on the principle of complete equity and respect for each other's legitimate interests so that the three countries may be forever bound together in the common cause of national construction and defense."[24] If necessary, Vietnam's equitable framework would be implemented by force in the pursuit of an Indochinese Federation deferent to Vietnamese interests.

Hanoi concluded that it could only achieve its objectives by eliminating the Khmer Rouge regime. It had already launched counteroffensive attacks deep within Kampuchea; yet based on the fear of provoking a Chinese response, it chose to limit the conflict and pursue a strategy of publicizing the brutal excesses of the Khmer regime, condemning of China for supporting it, and attempting to foster an internal uprising through a propaganda campaign.[25] Hanoi accused Kampuchea and Pol Pot of being a murderous, fascist clique and the enemy of the people. It also accused China of arming Kampuchea against Vietnam and denounced China as reactionary, expansionist, and hegemonist. However, the Vietnamese attempt to foster an internal coup in Phnom Penh was unsuccessful. The failure of an internal rebellion strategy, coupled with Chinese military and diplomatic aid to Kampuchea, caused Vietnam to take a course of direct intervention before Kampuchea could grow stronger militarily and diplomatically. This also impelled Vietnam to begin treaty negotiations with the Soviets to deter the possibility of direct intervention by China.[26]

In August and September of 1977, Soviet aircraft provided Vietnam with 200 T-62 tanks and numerous surface-to-air and antiship missiles, as well as Soviet technical advisors. Vietnam began a concerted propaganda campaign to falsely report nonexistent

---

[24]Ibid., 33.

[25]Ibid., 35.

[26]Gilks, 215.

122

internal uprisings in Phnom Penh to establish a pretext for its planned invasion. In

October 1977, fighting on the Kampuchean-Vietnamese border escalated. Pol Pot visited

China to solicit more military aid as well as a Chinese commitment to protect Kampuchea

from Vietnam. The latter was not obtained. China still desired a peaceful settlement to

the conflict, while at the same time wishing to ensure that Kampuchea was strong enough

to withstand Vietnamese pressure in pursuit of goals contrary to China's interest.[27] To

that end Deng hosted a secret meeting between the Vietnamese Deputy Premier Pham

Hung and Pol Pot; however, a compromise solution was not reached.

In November 1977, Le Duan led a delegation to Beijing to discuss Vietnam's

differing interests regarding relations with the Soviet Union and the creation of an

Indochinese federation; however, he was unable to receive Chinese acquiescence to

Vietnamese objectives. Beijing immediately dispatched a senior politburo member to

inform Phnom Penh of Vietnam's attempt to obtain concessions from China on

Kampuchea and to demonstrate Chinese determination to support Kampuchea, even at the

cost of completing Vietnam's final alignment with the Soviet Union. Miscalculating

China's interest and determination in maintaining an independent Kampuchea and failing

to achieve a negotiated settlement of its strategic objectives, Vietnam decided to resolve

the issue by force. In an attempt to compel Kampuchea to accede to its demands,

Vietnam initiated limited large scale attacks on Kampuchea. To support this overt

military effort, Vietnam also opened a political front, establishing the Kampuchean

National United Front for National Salvation (KNUFNS). China condemned the action

---

[27]Ibid., 180.

as "a fresh signal for launching armed aggression on a bigger scale to realize the strategy of an Indochinese Federation jointly planned by Vietnam and the Soviet Union."[28] Kampuchea accused Vietnam of attempting to annex Kampuchea and severed relations on 31 December 1977. With the assistance of Chinese military aid, the Kampuchean's were able to push the Vietnamese back to the original border by January 1978. Throughout the remainder of the year, battles waged without a decisive victor, both sides claiming victory.

On 3 November 1978, Vietnam and the Soviet Union concluded a Treaty of Friendship and Cooperation, further straining China's relationship with the two countries. This action, coupled with Soviet adventurism in Afghanistan, reinforced China's perceptions of a Soviet strategy of encirclement. The treaty was viewed by China as an offensive military alliance and a prelude to an imminent Vietnamese offensive in Kampuchea.[29] Deng Xiaoping labeled the treaty "a direct threat to the security and peace of Asia, the Pacific, and the world." The Chinese press labeled Vietnam as the "Cuba of the East," and referred to the two countries as "big hegemonist" and "little hegemonist." Deng sent Wang Dongxing (Vice Chairman of the CCP) to Phnom Penh to provide additional moral and material support to Kampuchea in the wake of the Soviet-Vietnamese treaty. Vietnam criticized the trip as being aimed at "seeking ways to prolong Kampuchea's horrible disaster in order to carry out Beijing's hegemonist scheme

---

[28]Ibid., 221.

[29]Ibid., 218.

124

in fighting Vietnam to the last Kampuchean citizen."[30] Meanwhile, the Soviet Union increased its infusion of arms and military advisors into Vietnam. Hanoi was concerned about the possibility of Chinese intervention in Kampuchea (as requested by Pol Pot already in November); however, China refused to make such a commitment, fearing that it might draw China into an Indochinese quagmire not unlike the experience of the United States. On 6 January 1979, despite reports of the impending full-scale invasion of Kampuchea by Vietnam, Deng Xiaoping ruled out an immediate intervention in the conflict. However, he did state that Vietnamese aggression in Kampuchea was part of a Soviet program of expansionism and a combined threat to China. He also stated that China "must one day be obliged to take measures contrary to its wishes for peace."[31]

On 25 December 1978, Vietnam invaded Kampuchea in force, employing over 200,000 troops. Despite previous suppression by the Khmer regime, Sihanouk was allowed to fly to Beijing to request Chinese support and then to the United Nations to appeal unsuccessfully to the Security Council for support in ejecting Vietnam from Kampuchea.[32] On 7 January 1979, Phnom Penh fell. The following day, the Vietnamese installed Heng Samrin announced the establishment of the People's Revolutionary Council of Kampuchea. Hanoi (as well as Moscow) immediately recognized the new government and hailed it as "the beginning of a new era in which the three nations on the

---

[30]Chen, 36.

[31]Chen, 37.

[32]Ibid., 37.

125

Indochinese peninsula will unite to build a new life in the spirit of absolute respect for one another's independence, sovereignty, and equality of mutual assistance."[33]

Hanoi portrayed the invasion as a legitimate act of self defense against Chinese sponsored aggression and as a humanitarian intervention against a genocidal regime. Beijing responded, stating that such a lawless aggression must be stopped. Vietnam responded by warning China and Thailand that no one can interfere in Kampuchea's internal affairs and by rapidly establishing control over most of Kampuchea, reducing the Khmer Rouge to conducting guerrilla operations out of the western jungle along the Thai border. On 12 January 1979, China issued a statement demanding an immediate cease-fire, the withdrawal of Vietnamese troops, and a negotiated settlement. At the same time it pledged its continued aid and support for Kampuchea. Additionally, Deng dispatched Deng Yingchao (Zhou's wife) to Phnom Penh to appraise the situation in the country. Meanwhile Thailand, fearful of the possibility of the war expanding into its border, reluctantly agreed to China's request to supply arms and material via Thailand to the remaining Khmer forces continuing to resist the Vietnamese. By the end of January, Pham Van Dong stated that the newly established PRK (People's Republic of Kampuchea), under the leadership of Heng Samrin, had accepted the occupation of Kampuchea by Vietnamese forces.

Escalating territorial disputes between China and Vietnam and disputes over the "Hoa" or overseas Chinese in Vietnam compounded the strategic issue of Kampuchea. China and Vietnam share a 797-mile land boundary, as well as the Gulf of Tonkin, and

---

[33]Gilks, 225.

both countries assert claims on the Paracel and Spratly Islands. Historically, no border disputes existed between the two countries. Incursions were made to gain influence and power, but not territory.[34] The border itself was not delimited until 1887, under a Sino-French convention. The arrangement failed to address the Gulf of Tonkin or the South China Sea.

Territorial disputes became a symptom of heightening tensions resulting from the complexities of the Sino-Soviet rift. The first identified disagreement between North Vietnam and China took place in 1974 over common points along the Sino-Vietnamese railway. North Vietnam argued that the boundary was mistakenly demarcated 300 meters inside its territory. Hanoi asked for an adjustment, which China summarily rejected. Hanoi also made claims against territory holding a key oil pipeline, as well as numerous other points on the frontier. Violent incidents took place between local authorities and residents on both sides.

Disagreement at an August 1974 conference over the Tonkin Gulf served only to intensify the border dispute. Vietnam changed an earlier position by claiming that the Gulf on Tonkin was delimited under the 1887 Treaty, giving Vietnam over 66 percent of the Gulf area. China refuted Vietnam's claim, arguing that the line in question was meant to delineate ownership of offshore islands and not to demarcate the sea boundary in the Gulf. In May 1977, at Youyiguan (Friendship Pass), over fifty Chinese railway workers were injured by Vietnamese soldiers. A week later, Vietnam unilaterally announced a 200-mile economic zone encompassing Chinese claimed islands in the Tonkin Gulf. By

---

[34]Chen, 40.

127

midyear, suspicious of the loyalty of ethnic Chinese, Vietnam initiated a campaign to purify its northern border. All Chinese and non-Vietnamese residents along the border were forcibly expelled. Rather than eliminating the problem as Vietnam had thought, the new policy served only to accelerate the frequency and intensity of border conflicts.

During negotiations held in October 1977, China proposed that both sides review the demarcation of the border in accordance with the Sino-French boundary accord of 1887 to come to a resolution of the dispute and to conclude a new boundary treaty between Vietnam and China. Vietnam refused, claiming that the Chinese precondition that Vietnam give up its claims over the Parcel and Spratly Archipelagoes was unacceptable. By 1978, Vietnam declined to conduct further negotiations on the boundary, claiming that it was too busy to negotiate.[35]

Of equal importance in the territorial dispute was the disagreement over the Paracel Islands (Xisha Islands to the Chinese and Hoang Sa to the Vietnamese) and the Spratly Islands (Nansha Islands to the Chinese and Troung Sa to the Vietnamese). The Paracels lie 160 miles southeast of the Chinese Hainan Islands and 225 miles east of Danang. The Spratly Islands, the more disputed of the two archipelagos, lie 540 miles south of the Paracels and 400 miles east of Saigon. The Spratly Islands are also claimed by the Philippines. The significance of both island chains is based on the perceptions of both countries' concept of sovereignty, the potential for vast deposits of oil beneath the ocean floor, and the strong sense of nationalism which followed an era of imperial domination. The islands were also of strategic interest to the Soviet Union, US, and

---

[35]Ibid., 49.

Japan due to their commanding positions astride key sea routes between the Pacific and Indian Oceans.

Chinese claims to both sets of islands are supported by history extending back to the Sung Dynasty. Historic records and legal precedent support this claim.[36] However, in 1931, France challenged China's sovereignty over both the Paracel and Spratly Islands on behalf of its protectorate, Vietnam. In 1933, the French occupied the islands under Chinese protest. They were then occupied by the Japanese from 1939 to 1945. In 1946 the Chinese Nationalist Government of Taiwan occupied several of the islands only to be removed by Peoples Republic of China forces in 1950. After the peace treaty with Japan was signed, both China and Vietnam reasserted their claims to the islands. In 1956, the Democratic Peoples Republic of Vietnam acknowledged that the "Xisha and Nansha islands were historically part of Chinese Territory." Also in 1956, Taiwan sent forces to occupy the Spratly islands. In 1958 North Vietnam's Premier Pham Van Dong again endorsed China's claim to the islands.

By 1961, under protest from the Chinese, Saigon announced the incorporation of the Paracels into Vietnam. The interest in the islands increased after United Nations oceanographic studies in the late 1960s assessed that large oil reserves where likely in the area. In 1973 South Vietnam occupied one of the Spratly Islands and negotiated contracts for oil exploration with several foreign oil companies. Saigon also unilaterally incorporated several of the islands into Vietnam. This compelled the Chinese to occupy the Paracels and to remove the Vietnamese by force in 1974. Saigon responded by

---

[36]Ibid., 44.

occupying several islands of the Spratlys. Beijing called Saigon's action an invasion and reiterated China's claims to both chains. Taipei also issued statements reasserting its sovereignty over the islands and officially protested both the Vietnamese and Philippine claims.

In 1975 North Vietnamese troops occupied islands previously garrisoned by South Vietnam and the new government of Vietnam published maps which delimited the Paracels and Spratly Islands within Vietnamese territory. In 1977, Pham Van Dong reversed his previous statement acknowledging China's historical rights to both island chains, claiming that the original understanding was a result of wartime exigencies. This reversal was a direct result of the deteriorating Sino-Vietnamese relationship. Subsequent negotiations on the islands yielded no progress. By 10 November 1978, China issued a strong warning to Vietnam regarding the ongoing border conflicts:

> It is absolutely by no means accidental that the Vietnamese authorities stirred up disturbances along the Sino-Vietnamese border on the eve of their intensified aggression against Kampuchea and their conclusion of a military alliance with the Soviet Union. . . . We have to question the Vietnamese authorities: What are you up to? How far will you go? . . . The Chinese people are determined to safeguard their sovereignty and territorial integrity. . . . We sternly warn the Vietnamese authorities: Draw back your criminal band and stop the provocation and intrusions along the Chinese-Vietnamese border.[37]

Contributing to the rapid deterioration of relations between China and Vietnam in 1975 was the issue of overseas Chinese in Vietnam. Ethnic Chinese have lived in Vietnam since the Sung Dynasty in the thirteenth century. The turmoil of the opium war in the mid-nineteenth century caused many Chinese to flee to Vietnam, where relative

---

[37]Ibid., 50.

stability and economic prosperity existed. The Chinese rapidly assumed dominant positions within the Vietnamese economy, yet they were never fully assimilated into Vietnamese culture. The Chinese maintained there own ethnic identity, establishing their own schools, newspapers, hospitals, and sports clubs. Nongovernmental organizations (Bangs) organized the Vietnamese Chinese community. Despite their wealth and organization, they possessed no political power.

After the fall of the South Vietnamese government, the new communist regime immediately sought transform the capitalist economy and society in the South. Many ethnic Chinese, by virtue of their economic position in key industries, were targeted as monopolists. The unification of Vietnam and subsequent political, economic, and social transformation of the South resulted in the liquidation of Chinese capital beginning with the anti-comprador bourgeoisie movement in 1975. The effect of these policies was the confiscation of Chinese property and assets by the new regime. These policies were not specifically aimed at Chinese, but because of their economic success, they bore the brunt of the transition from capitalism to socialism. Currency reform in 1975 wiped out the Chinese business class. This process was repeated in 1978 when the prospect of war gave impetus to the government to assert stronger control of the economy and to disenfranchise ethnic Chinese whose loyalty was suspect.[38]

The Chinese, having lost their wealth and businesses, were left with no means of earning a living. Consequently, they became easy targets for resettlement under Vietnam's five year economic plan which called for the creation of "new economic

---

[38]Gilks, 193.

131

zones" in the countryside. The purpose of the policy was to redistribute the labor force from the city to the country, so that displaced capitalists and the unemployed could move into agriculture to produce food for the country. It is estimated that six million people were forced out of cities in the South and into the new economic zones, of which 300-350 thousand were ethnic Chinese.[39] Because of a lack of preparation, these newly created areas lacked sufficient food, shelter, and medical support to accommodate the large number of displaced persons. Consequently, the harsh conditions caused great hardship. It is estimated that by 1975, over 200,000 ethnic Chinese fled over the border into China, further exacerbating border tensions.

In March 1978, the new regime conducted another mass campaign of socialist transformation for the stated purpose of "eliminating the private ownership of industry and commerce, building and expanding the socialist market, stabilizing prices, currency, production and peoples livelihoods, and strengthening political security."[40] All goods and businesses of capitalist traders were "purchased" or confiscated by the government, which repeated the raids, inspections, and confiscation of the anti-comprador bourgeoisie movement of 1975. In May 1978, Vietnam's second currency reform, designed to facilitate socialist transformation and to wipe out capitalist profiteers wiped out the remainder of the Chinese business and entrepreneurial class, most of which were sent to the new economic zones.

---

[39]Chen, 59.

[40]Ibid., 62-63.

As a result of Vietnam's social and economic policies, many refugees fled

Vietnam. Over 85 percent were ethnic Chinese. Additionally, Vietnam forcibly expelled

ethnic Chinese from the northern border. As a result, significant fighting was erupting

along the Sino-Vietnamese border. In May 1977, Vietnam officially sanctioned the

exodus by allowing anyone wishing to return to China to do so, increasing the cumulative

numbers of refugees fleeing Vietnam to over 100,000. The culmination of Chinese

fleeing Vietnam in the South via boat and the forced repatriation of ethnic Chinese in the

North resulted in the condemnation of Vietnam by the Beijing. China warned Vietnam to

"stop the erroneous policy of ostracizing, persecuting, and expelling Chinese residents-

otherwise the Vietnam government should bear full responsibility for all the

consequences arising from these unwarranted measures."[41] Vietnam responded by

denying the existence of Chinese "nationals" in Vietnam. At the same time, propaganda

portrayed them as fifth columnists. China signaled its disapproval by conducting a naval

and air show of force off of the Gulf of Haiphong. Three days later Beijing decided to

evacuate Chinese from Vietnam, sending ships to Haiphong and Saigon to receive and

transport ethnic Chinese back to China. Hanoi accused China of distorting the situation.

On 7 June 1978, Deng accused Vietnam of maltreating Chinese residents and

China itself, linking the Kampuchean and ethnic Chinese crisis as elements of a

coordinated policy of aggression directed at China.[42] Negotiations over the evacuation of

Chinese from Vietnam were deadlocked over procedures and over the time allowed for

---

[41]Ibid., 64-65.

[42]Gilks, 200.

133

the two Chinese boats to enter into Vietnamese ports and embark the overseas Chinese. On 16 June, Vietnam refused China's request of establish a Consulates-General in Ho Chi Minh City (Saigon). China retaliated by ordering the closure of three Vietnamese consulates in Guangzhou, Kumming, and Nanning. Additionally, China recalled its ambassador, ostensibly "because of poor health."[43]

On 29 June 1978, Vietnam, under the sponsorship of the Soviet Union, joined the COMCON (Council for Economic Mutual Assistance). China responded by ending all aid to Vietnam, withdrawing 880 advisors, and accusing Vietnam of "creating a foul atmosphere of vilifying and inciting antagonism against China."[44] On 11 July 1978, the Chinese People's Daily reported:

> It has become quite clear that the border conflict between Vietnam and Kampuchea is by no means accidental. This conflict, together with the Vietnamese authorities' anti-China acts, including the persecution and expulsion of Chinese residents in Vietnam and the using of the question of overseas Chinese to disrupt the relations between China and Southeast Asian nations, forms a component of the whole plot. In this plot, the Soviet superpower, with its own hegemonistic aims, provides cover and support for the Vietnamese authorities' regional hegemonism, while the Vietnamese authorities were as a junior partner for the Soviet Union. . . . People have seen one expression of this style in Cuba and now see another manifestation in Vietnam.[45]

By the end of the month, over 150,000 Chinese were forcibly repatriated from northern Vietnam to China.[46] In the south, as part of an International Red Cross agreement, Taiwan evacuated an additional 1,500. As a result of the escalation in the level of the

---

[43]Chen, 65.

[44]Gilks, 206.

[45]Ibid., 207.

[46]Chen, 65.

conflict with Kampuchea, Vietnam adopted a hard-line policy in conducting repatriation negotiations with China. Consequently, on 28 July 1978, after nineteen failed sessions, negotiations between the two countries on evacuation broke down, and China ordered the two evacuation ships to return empty.

At this stage, high tensions on both sides and the threat of war caused each to militarily reinforce its border areas. Hanoi accused the Chinese of creating the crisis by enticing 170,000 Hoa Chinese to return to China. Furthermore, Hanoi labeled overseas Chinese Comprador Bourgeoisie and accused them of being under the influence of Western imperialist as "foreign yellow-raced capitalists to exploit the Vietnamese people."[47] Hanoi also stated that the struggle against the Hoa comprador bourgeoisie was a class struggle and a struggle for national liberation.

China countered by accusing the Soviets of instigating the resident issue as part of a strategy to encircle China. The Chinese Renmin Ribo repeatedly accused the Soviets of creating hegemonism in Southeast Asia and of advising Vietnam to turn the overseas Chinese against China. Hanoi responded by claiming that China was "assisting the Hoa Bourgeoisie, causing difficulties and obstacles to Vietnam's socialist transformation and socialist construction, in the Chinese scheme of carrying out big nation hegemonism and big nation expansionism to oppose Vietnam's sovereignty and independence."[48]

The increase in Sino-Vietnamese border incidents reflected the escalation of the Kampuchean-Vietnamese crisis. By September of 1978, Hanoi anticipated war with

---

[47]Ibid., 66.

[48]Ibid, 67.

135

China and began to condition its population through propaganda stressing "traditional Vietnamese values of patriotism and independence that had coped with the big nation expansionism and hegemonism of the Han feudalists." At the same time, Vietnam attempted to improve its position on the border by occupying strategically important areas of disputed territories and expelling additional Chinese residents there.[49] Vietnam also signaled a warning to "imperialists and international reactionaries" that their invasion would be defeated. In October 1978, China responded in kind, issuing a formal protest over Vietnamese encroachments on the Chinese border and signaling stronger warnings: should Vietnam "obdurately go their own way continuing to act provocatively on the border . . . and continuing to threaten the Chinese with war, they will certainly be victims of their own evil deeds."[50] Published statements also proclaimed that "Soviet big power hegemonism and the Vietnamese authorities' regional hegemonism have dovetailed and served each other on the common basis of aggression and expansionism . . . emboldened by Soviet backing the swell headed Vietnamese authorities regard the great Chinese people as susceptible to bullying. . . . We sternly warn the Vietnamese authorities: draw back your criminal hand stretched into Chinese territory."[51]

China debated for considerable time how to handle the Vietnamese problem regarding territorial disputes, strategic alignment with the Soviets, Kampuchea, and the expulsion of ethnic Chinese. Chen argues that China's final decision to invade Vietnam

---

[49]Gilks, 221.

[50]Ibid., 218.

[51]Ibid., 218-219.

was not based on miscalculation or confusion but rather long consideration and repeated debate. In a conference originally scheduled to last three days, the CCP Central Work Conference and the Third Plenum of the Eleventh Congress debated for thirty-five days the future of economic and social policy, as well as direct intervention in Kampuchea. Though determined to punish Vietnam, the Politburo decided not to directly intervene in Kampuchea. According to Geng Biao, a participant, four considerations weighed against such a course of action:

1. China was a socialist state and oppossed sending troops abroad. To do so might threaten other countries in Southeast Asia.

2. International support for Kampuchea stemmed largely from the fact that it was a victim of Vietnamese aggression; if China also sent troops, it would undermine this sentiment.

3. China risked being bogged down, and moreover, lacked sufficient strength to fight such a war of attrition while trying to carry out the Four Modernizations.

4. For these reasons, the Soviet Union wanted China to intervene. If the war spread to Vietnam, the Soviets would have a reason to dispatch troops from the north to conduct a pincer attack. If China precipitated a major conflict with the Soviet Union, it might jeopardize hoped for investments and loans from Japan and the West for the modernization plan. [52]

Yet Chinese credibility as an ally was a stake, as was its determination to halt Soviet-sponsored Vietnamese expansion in Indochina. Accordingly, China chose to continue military and economic aid to Kampuchea. The crisis became urgent once the Vietnamese concluded a treaty of friendship and cooperation with the Soviets. The Soviet naval presence in Cam Ranh Bay and Hanoi's decision to eject Pol Pot by force was exacerbated by the failure to settle the Chinese refugee and border problems.

---

[52]Ibid., 221.

Consequently, China was determined to teach its "small ungrateful brother in the South" a lesson.

By December 1978, China had moved additional troops to its border with Vietnam as a result of Vietnamese encroachments in Guangxi and Yunnan. During the Central Workers Conference Deng laid out his rationale for a punitive war against Vietnam:

1. The action was a limited self defensive counterattack on Vietnam.

2. The Soviets were incapable of mounting a large scale attack against China given their military priorities in Europe. Any medium strength Soviet response in Xinjiang, Inner Mongolia, or Heilongjiang could be managed.

3. A limited punitive war would not interrupt the Four Modernizations program.

4. A Chinese invasion and subsequent withdrawal would demonstrate China's control of the situation.

5. Any end result would not end in a great victory or defeat.

6. Such a demonstration of resolve was less likely to invite international censure compared to a direct intervention in Kampuchea. [53]

At the conclusion of the Third Plenum, China issued an explicit warning to Vietnam, stating:

China . . . will never attack unless it is attacked, but if it is attacked, it will certainly counter attack. China means what it says. We wish to warn the Vietnamese authorities that if they count on Moscow's support to seek a foot after gaining an inch and to continue to act in an unbridled fashion, they will decidedly meet with the punishment they deserve. We are telling you this now. Don't complain later that we have not given you clear warning in advance. [54]

---

[53]Chen, 87.

[54]Ibid., 89.

At the end of December, train service between the two countries was suspended. On 1 January 1979, the Chinese ambassador and military attaché to Vietnam were recalled to Beijing.

The decision to take military action against Vietnam was also linked to Sino-US relations. In an effort to strengthen China against a Soviet threat, Deng accelerated the process of normalization with the United States by delivering a Chinese draft joint communiqué proposal to Washington on 4 December 1978. On 11 December 1978, four days after Vietnam had invaded Kampuchea, Deng received an invitation from President Carter to visit Washington as part of the establishment of formal diplomatic recognition scheduled to take effect on 1 January 1979. During his subsequent visit between 28 January and 5 February, Deng emphasized the linkage between Vietnamese aggression in Kampuchea and Soviet expansionism in Indochina and explicitly discussed with Carter the likely necessity for China to conduct a limited punitive war against Vietnam.[55] Carter attempted to discourage such a move, but expressed no strong objections. Deng was able to secure wording in a subsequently released joint communiqué expressing shared Sino-US interest in opposing hegemony. Prior to his departure from the United States, Deng reiterated Chinese warnings in a television interview, stating that Beijing might take military action against Vietnam because of its aggression in Kampuchea and its provocative border incidents with China. No public condemnation or rejection resulted from the statement. On his way back to China via Japan, Deng again issued a similar

---

[55]Ibid., 91.

warning, and in doing so strengthened the perception that Vietnam and its Soviet ally were opposed by the combined strength of China, the United States, and Japan.

Hanoi responded by attacking Deng's trip to the United States as a "sinister policy of ganging with United States imperialism against Vietnam." It also stated that "If they (China) want to learn a lesson, let them learn it from their US masters."[56] By this time the Soviets built up a small naval force off of the Vietnamese coast. Despite this signal of Soviet interest in Vietnam to China, war plans for the punitive invasion on Vietnam were finalized on Deng's return on 8 February 1979. Between 9-12 February, Deng made his proposal to the Chinese Central Military Commission. Based on the observations made during his recent trip to the United States and Japan, Deng concluded that the present time offered the best opportunity to teach Vietnam an lesson.[57]

Chen asserts that the principles of prudence and restraint were demonstrated by the Chinese in their deliberations on Vietnam. Deng's concept of the nature of the war was one that was a self-defensive counterattack, limited in time and space, and also limited to ground fighting only. The objective of the war was to give Vietnam a lesson. Vietnam had made claims of being the third largest military power in the world, offending China's perception of its political and military dominance of the region. Vietnam had invaded Kampuchea contrary to China's announced interests and had expelled Chinese residents. Additionally, Vietnam had committed numerous border incursions against China, killing Chinese civilians and soldiers alike. Therefore, China

---

[56]Ibid., 92.

[57]Ibid., 92.

would fight back but would refrain from occupying one inch of Vietnamese territory. Once Chinese forces had achieved their limited objectives (never fully disclosed), China would withdraw.

Though all of the above factors contributed to China's ultimate decision to take military action, China's predominant concern was its perception of encirclement by Soviet client states. China's decision was one of last resort, given its recognition that its military lacked the modern weapons and equipment, mobility and logistical support necessary to conduct sustained operations beyond its borders. Additionally, China could not achieve its ambitious modernization programs in the wake of a general war.

The situation became an unstoppable crescendo as events rapidly unfolded. On 10 February, Pravda accused China of massing troops on the Vietnamese border. On 12 February, Deputy Premier Li Xiannian stated to a visiting Pakistani delegation that Vietnam should not ignore Chinese warnings.[58] That same day, Vietnam's Nhan Dan published a warning to China not to touch Vietnam. On 14 February, the Sino-Soviet treaty expired. On 16 February, China issued its final warning to Vietnam, making a strongest protest against Vietnam's incursions into Chinese territory. Then, on 17 February, the Chinese struck. The following day, Vietnam and Kampuchea concluded a treaty of peace, friendship, and cooperation providing for mutual assistance in national defense and reconstruction, legitimizing Vietnam's occupation and realizing the ambition of establishing an Indochinese federation (albeit by force), and now in the face of war with China.

---

[58]Ibid., 93.

Though limited, China did commit thirty-one divisions along two fronts (approximately 330,000 troops supported by 1,200 tanks or 10 percent of its overall military capability).[59] Vietnam's military was only one-third of China's force in size due to its commitments in Kampuchea and Laos (approximately 175,000 and 100,000, respectively); however, it was capable and experienced. China's initial efforts were hindered by difficult terrain and its shortfalls in logistical sustainment. Its employment of large units put it at a disadvantage relative to the smaller more mobile Vietnamese. Nevertheless, China achieved its initial objectives by 22 February, capturing Lao Cai and Cao Bang, dominating the approaches to Hanoi, only eighty-five miles to the South.

The Soviets issued a statements citing its treaty obligations to Vietnam, urged China to stop before it was too late, and demanded an immediate Chinese withdraw from Vietnam. On 19 February, China publicly repeated its message that the war was limited and punitive in nature and that China would withdraw once it had achieved its objectives. On 21 February, the Soviets moved an aircraft carrier and a destroyer to the South China sea and began to airlift of arms to Vietnam via Calcutta. They continued to demand that China withdraw its troops, more so to boost Vietnam's morale than to signal any potential Soviet escalation of the conflict. Despite its rhetoric, Soviet officials quietly assured Western and Asian diplomats that it would not intervene provided that China kept the fighting limited.[60] On 25 February, China stated that it had no intention of moving its forces into Hanoi.

---

[59]Ibid., 101.

[60]Ibid., 110.

142

At the United Nations, the United States requested a special session to debate the problem in Indochina and to address its implications for security in the region. The Soviets warned that it would not support a resolution which failed to condemn China and call for a Chinese withdraw from Vietnam. On 23 February, the Soviet Union and Czechoslovakia submitted a draft resolution condemning China for its aggression, demanding the withdrawal of Chinese forces, full reparations for Vietnamese war damages, and arms embargo against China. China countered by criticizing the Soviets for encouraging Vietnamese border aggression against China and its invasion of Kampuchea. On 24 February, China submitted a draft resolution calling for the withdrawal of all Vietnamese forces from Kampuchea.

Between 27 February and 5 March, the war centered on Lang Son, resulting in heavy casualties on both sides. On 5 March, Chinese forces captured Lang Son, controlling approaches into the Red River delta, and demonstrating their ability to threaten Ho Chi Minh City. On capturing this final objective, China announced that it would begin its promised withdraw, relieving the Soviets from the unpalatable choice of either entering the war or abandoning its ally. China warned Vietnam not to interfere with the withdrawal or face a renewed Chinese offensive. Vietnam complied and Chinese forces completed their withdraw on 16 March.

Despite the significant losses sustained on both sides, Deng claimed the operation a success. What was achieved beyond a demonstration of Chinese determination to send an unmistakable signal to Vietnam that it could not pursue its own interests in Indochina without weighing Chinese interests is debatable. China ultimately was able to undermine

Vietnam's quest to establish an Indochinese Federation. Yet China was unable to completely destroy Vietnam's military forces or to force a Vietnamese withdraw from Kampuchea, though it did alleviate some of the military pressure on Kampuchea. Neither, as history would bear out, did the conflict end the border clashes or influence Hanoi's policy regarding Chinese residents. China did gain credibility and tacit support from the ASEAN nations in its decision to oppose Vietnamese expansion in Asia. Furthermore, it also identified the limits to the price that the Soviets were willing to pay to expand their influence in Asia via client states. More indirectly, the war demonstrated the value of Sino-US rapprochement and the necessity of modernizing its military forces in terms of weaponry, strategy, and doctrine.

China was unwilling to expand the scope of the conflict due to the adverse impact that it would have on its economy and fear of a general war which might include the Soviet Union. Continued opposition to Soviet and Vietnamese influence in Kampuchea via support for the Khmer Rouge rebels against the Heng Samrin government demonstrated Chinas resolve at an acceptable cost. Attempts to establish an Asian united front of military, political and economic pressure against the Vietnamese occupation of Kampuchea would continue to be undermined by the barbarous nature of the Khmer Rouge under Pol Pot. Though China was appalled at Khmer atrocities, the Khmer Rouge were China's only tool to fight the Vietnamese and their client regime. (This would later change with the "retirement" of Pol Pot and subsequent ASEAN endorsement of a Kampuchean coalition government under Sihanouk in 1981.)

China's conflict with Vietnam was more complicated than its previous conflict with India or its intervention in Korea. The conflict with Vietnam involved competing territorial claims, repeated border clashes, the maltreatment of resident overseas Chinese, competition for the leadership of Asia with an expanding Soviet sphere of influence. The last two factors played the greatest role in China's decision to conduct a punitive war against Vietnam. Chinese objectives, as seen in previous conflicts, were in the context of a triangular relationship involving a neighboring state and a great power, in this case the Soviet Union. Given its limited nature, it is unlikely that China believed that it would secure a Vietnamese withdraw from Kampuchea. However, the Chinese invasion demonstrated its ability and determination to use force if necessary to assert its geopolitical interests in the region and as a warning to deter future adventures.

CHAPTER 6

CONCLUSION

> The case material reveals that perhaps the most important single precipitating factor in the out break of war is misperception. Such distortion may manifest itself in four different ways: in a leader's image of himself; a leader's view of his adversary's character; a leader's view of his adversary's intentions toward himself; and, finally, a leader's view of his adversary's capabilities and power.[1]
>
> John G. Stoessinger

The stated objective of this study was to determine the veracity of Chinese interests and objectives as identified in the Chinese white paper and to identify consistent patterns of Chinese national and strategic thought with respect to national interest, foreign relations, conflict and how that thought is translated into policy and articulated to potential adversaries. Implied in the above inquiry is a determination of the employment of deception in China's conduct of foreign policy. What conclusions can be drawn from the case studies examined?

First, the foregoing case studies clearly demonstrate that China consistently attempted to convey its national interests to its adversaries and repeatedly warned them of the repercussions of what was genuinely perceived as aggressive behavior directly threatening the security of China. At no time did China employ deception in its diplomacy. In each instance, China's adversaries consciously chose to ignore those warnings out of hubris or contempt of China. China will likely continue to candidly express its concerns and interests in the future. Therefore, in the future, as in the past, it

---

[1]John G. Stoessinger, *Why Nations go to War*, 3d ed. (New York: St. Martin's Press, 1982), 209.

would be imprudent to ignore or dismiss diplomatic and military signaling by the Chinese.

Second, each major conflict addressed was not initiated by China but by one of its neighbors acting independently or in concert with an outside power, to change the regional status quo. Archival evidence clearly demonstrates that the Korean conflict was conceived by Kim and Stalin, not Mao. Mao was left with a fait accompli after the fact and was compelled to intervene to protect China's vulnerable industrial base in Manchuria from an openly hostile and aggressive MacArthur.

The 1962 conflict with India was a precipitated by India's domestic political agenda and aggressive actions under Nehru's Forward Policy. China clearly attempted to peacefully negotiate a satisfactory resolution to the dispute and signaled a willingness to accept the status quo or a reasonable quid pro quo. India's jingoistic intransigence and offensive actions left China with no alternative than to counter attack to defend Chinese territory and interests.

The 1979 conflict with Vietnam was a response to Vietnam's attempt to establish, by force, an Indochinese federation subordinate to Vietnam and aligned with the Soviet Union, contrary to Chinese interests. Soviet supported Vietnamese aggression both in Kampuchea and on China's southern border dictated a strong Chinese response, despite the risks of incurring a wider war.

With the exception of the 1962 Sino-Indian war, regional conflict was not the proximate cause of Chinese intervention but rather the medium for confrontation with perceived aggressive, outside powers. China's involvement in regional conflict was

147

always predicated on two defensive objectives: to prevent either a direct assault on Chinese territorial integrity or a perceived threat to its territorial integrity (such as in the Indian and Korean conflicts), or to prevent other powers from establishing a military presence along its vulnerable borders which could threaten China's territorial integrity in the future (such as the Soviet presence in Vietnam and, by proxy, in India, Laos, and Kampuchea). China did not engage in conflict to expand its power or achieve hegemony in the region but it did so to prevent others from expanding their power or achieving hegemony in the region. This has important ramifications with respect to the ongoing territorial disputes in the South China Sea.

Third, each conflict transcended the regional actors involved. Beyond amicable relations, China's neighbors were not as important themselves as was the context of their relationships with other outside powers which were strong enough to threaten China. An independent Korea and or even a divided Korea posed little threat to China. However, a Korea united by force of arms by a powerful country like the United States posed a grave threat to Chinese security, particularly given US support of the Nationalists during the civil war and the stationing of US forces in Taiwan in the 1950s.

Vietnam's challenge to the regional status quo and its treatment of ethnic Chinese was certainly of concern to China; however, these issues in themselves were not the proximate cause of China's punitive war with Vietnam. Vietnam, even leading a united and subordinate Indochinese Federation, posed little threat to China. However, a united Indochinese Federation under the influence of the Soviet Union via a surrogate or client state represented a serious strategic threat requiring action. China's national interest and

148

security was threatened not by a neighbor but by its relationship with an outside power, either the United States or the Soviet Union. Both superpowers had directly violated China's sovereignty and territorial integrity in the past and pursued policies inimical to Chinese interests during the setting of each conflict. Care should be taken in future crises to consider subjective Chinese perceptions of third party actors in a given conflict.

Fourth, in each of the conflicts addressed, China repeatedly attempted to resolve the disputes via negotiation and gradually escalated its responses. In the Korean conflict, this mechanism was denied as a result of neither the United States nor the United Nations recognizing China; however, China made its willingness to negotiate a settlement of the Korean conflict known along with its willingness to fight to maintain a buffer state between itself and its perceived antagonists.

In the case of India, extreme nationalist rhetoric and political ineptitude denied Nehru the ability to negotiate a reasonable compromise or even an arrangement favorable to India. Though in a position to drive the dispersed and weak Indian outposts and patrols from its territorial claims, China repeatedly attempted to negotiate a settlement, offering Nehru a face-saving way out of his predicament, even after India had repeatedly provoked hostile clashes north of the McMahon Line.

In the Sino-Vietnamese conflict, it was Vietnam who chose to sever negotiations, for "lack of time." Though unsuccessful, China attempted to mediate the conflict between Vietnam and Kampuchea. Though invited by Kampuchea, China declined to send its troops or intervene directly with military force. In each case, it was not China but its antagonists who refused to negotiate or broke off negotiations prior to the

149

escalation of the conflict. Also in each case, China's antagonists mistook Chinese restraint for weakness. China will likely continue to prefer the negotiating table to the battlefield because of the diplomatic and economic risks involved, provided the status quo is respected in the interim.

Fifth, China consistently demonstrated restraint after securing its limited, defensive objectives in the interest of protecting itself against perceived threats to its territorial integrity, even when in a position to militarily exploit the relative weakness of its opponent. After securing status quo defensive lines along the 38th Parallel in 1951, China agreed to engage in negotiations with the UN at Kaesong and to suspend, in advance, the fighting during those negotiations. It was General Ridgeway, supported by the Joint Chiefs, the State Department, and President Truman, who insisted that military operations continue during the negotiations.[2]

After securing its legitimate border claims and demonstrating its military capability to expand beyond them in both the Indian and Vietnamese conflicts, China unilaterally withdrew. Though China possesses a relatively unsophisticated military and will continue to do so for years to come (despite ongoing efforts at modernization), China has always possessed the sheer power of size to aggressively overwhelm its neighbors if it had an inclination to do so. Yet it has not. There exist no reasons to conclude that it will do so in the future.

Sixth, Chinese decisions to employ military force were borne of defensive considerations rather than offensive ambitions and were not made in haste or alacrity but

---

[2]Bevin Alexander, *Korea, the First War We Lost* (New York: Hippocrene Books, 1986), 430.

only after considerable debate within the Politburo. Its ultimate decisions to intervene were based on a rational and objective examination of the relative cost and benefits to military intervention and its alternatives. As seen prior to intervention in Korea, contentious debate between Zhou and Lin on one side and Peng and Gao on the other took place prior to Mao's decision. In the Aksai Chin and NEFA, China did not execute a counteroffensive until 38 months after the first clash with Indian forces in Chinese held territory and 22 months after India began implementing its Forward Policy.

In Vietnam, China gave its lesson to Hanoi without "occupying one inch of Vietnamese territory" (or Kampuchean territory). Its final decision was made only after extensive internal debate and external consultation with the US. Based on available documentation and memoirs, this pattern was consistent regardless of the senior leadership, Mao or Deng. The current leadership under Jiang Zemin is even more collaborative in its policy formulation.

Seventh, China consistently demonstrated pragmatism and realism in its foreign policy. When necessary, China subordinated ideology to geopolitical necessity and regional and international consensus. China has repeatedly demonstrated its ability to sustain the global and regional balance of power in its engagement and disengagement of the superpowers and other members of the international community. Based on the success of post-Tiananmen diplomatic initiatives, China will likely continue this approach.

Eighth, China attempted to facilitate a face saving way out of conflict for its adversaries when they unwisely limited their options by extreme rhetoric or by subjecting

151

those options to the vagaries of public opinion and political opposition. In Korea, China provided ample warning for both the US and the UN to reexamine their expanded objective of reunifying the peninsula. China also signaled that it could accept ROK forces north of the 38th parallel, though not US forces. Additionally, it could be argued that the Chinese armies' sudden disappearance after first making contact with US forces south of the Yalu was aimed at giving the US the opportunity to withdraw before becoming decisively engaged by the Chinese army. China's willingness to accept the status quo and defer border negotiations with Nehru until after Indian domestic passions receded, as well as offering congratulatory notes on the occasion of India's tenth national anniversary is another example of providing "face" to its adversaries. At a minimum, China has displayed a willingness to accept an unpalatable status quo based on "present realities" and a willingness to postpone the final negotiations of difficult issues at a more domestically opportune time for its opponent. It is conceded that in the case of Vietnam, no examples can be found to support this conclusion, likely due to the simple fact that unlike the West or India, the North Vietnamese regime was not subject to an opposition party or an independent press.

Ninth, China was always prepared to accept severe national hardship in order to defend its legitimate security interests, risking both the potential rise of internal reactionary forces and war with the United States in Korea and with the Soviets in the Indian and Vietnamese conflicts. Despite the internal turbulence of consolidating the revolution, the failure of the Great Leap Forward and the chaos of the Cultural Revolution, China embarked on defensive policies which risked war with each superpower. In each case, China consciously weighed the risks of escalation involving a superpower and the adverse impact that it would have on China during a period of significant internal weakness. Therefore, should internal instability arise in China again during a future crisis, it should not be viewed as an opportunity which can be exploited or perceived as being more important relative to China's perceived strategic and geopolitical interests.

Tenth, China did not use the perceived expansion of other powers as a pretext to secure its own "expansionist" aims. China did not use the Korean, Indian or Indochinese wars as a pretext to establish military power projection bases within the territory of its neighbors or clients. It established no permanent Chinese bases in Korea. It established no forward presence on territory undisputedly belonging to India when it had a clear opportunity to do so. It refused Kampuchea's invitation for Chinese troops and occupied no Vietnamese territory. Therefore, claims of future Chinese aggression based on historic regional aggression and expansionism beyond its borders are not supported by post-1949 history or policy. It is conceded that China has and will continue to use military force to maintain its control over provinces, such as Tibet and Xinjiang, and is prepared to use force to maintain the status quo (One China, two systems) in Taiwan and the South China Sea.

Finally, China since 1949 has primarily concerned itself with internal economic development and security issues, rather than external expansion or hegemony. Indeed, these priorities have been interrupted by the real or perceived aggression from China's neighbors or an outside power attempting to alter the status quo.

153

It is not argued here that China's previous conduct and motivations in foreign policy are deterministic of future motivation and policy. It is only to demonstrate the fallacy of selectively attempting to use China's international behavior in the past, without analyzing of events from a Chinese perspective which compelled that behavior, as a means to support assertions that China is inherently expansionist, hegemonistic, and not to be trusted.

Chinese national behavior in its relations with its neighbors has generally been consistent with its stated foreign policy goals as articulated in the Five Principles of Peaceful Coexistence: respect for territorial integrity and sovereignty, equality and mutual benefit, nonaggression, noninterference in the internal affairs of others, and the peaceful resolution of disputes. Specific exceptions under equally specific circumstances can be made to refute this assertion, but they cannot objectively be accepted as representative of the general pattern of Chinese foreign policy as a whole. Clearly the goals of mutual respect for territorial integrity and the peaceful resolution of disputes are limited by the degree to which an adversary agrees to reciprocate such a policy. Conflicts derived from territorial disputes, by their very nature, can represent either offensive or defensive behaviors, depending upon one's point of view. From a realist perspective, China, like any other nation, will ultimately act in accordance with perceived national interest and security dictates, particularly in the face of real or perceived aggression. Given China's historic experience with aggressive, foreign powers in the late nineteenth century and early twentieth century, it is clear that the maintenance of its territorial integrity and sovereignty is paramount.

154

This first requirement applies to its vulnerable provinces along its periphery of the mainland, such as Tibet and Xinjiang as it does the center. Equally important, it applies to Taiwan. Consequently, China will likely risk war, to prevent a fully independent Taiwan or the concept of "two Chinas" or any other separatist evolutions, regardless of the cost. As China has frequently stated, "Sovereignty cannot be negotiated." This closely relates to the second imperative: noninterference in the internal affairs of others. When assessed from the Chinese perspective, the current situation with respect to Taiwan is born directly of interference by outside powers, first Japan in 1895, and then the United States in 1950. Additionally, any objective examination of Chiang Kai Shek and the Kuomintang governance (as well as successive governments prior to 1995) reveals a degree of authoritarianism, repression, and corruption no less culpable than that found under the Chinese communist regime. Realist United States strategic and political requirements may objectively justify and even dictate its support for an independent Taiwan, but history and international law cannot.

Historic arguments couched in terms of normative values, such as self-determination and democracy, conveniently neglect to address these historic realities and are more often than not political realism cloaked in the veil of political idealism. Chinese claims to islands in the South China Sea are no more hegemonistic than US claims on the islands of Hawaii made during the same period. This is not to endorse China's claims or position on Taiwan today or to excuse its record on human rights: it is only to emphasize that, when viewed from a Chinese perspective, there are legitimate arguments which support their position and highlight real contradictions in opposing Western points of

155

view. These arguments must not necessarily be conceded in terms of policy concessions; however, they must be clearly understood to minimize unanticipated responses based on a misperception of Chinese "aggression." Due consideration of genuine Chinese perceptions of threat and legitimate national interest must be made.

China is more secure from external threats now than at any other period since 1949. Its greatest threat remains the internal ethnic and political aspirations of its diverse people, the latter a threat to the current regime more than to the national entity. Consequently, China's focus will continue to be on internal political and economic development rather than external hegemony. China is currently pursuing objectives clearly identified in its White Paper on National Defense and in concord with its proposed security paradigm of the Five Principles of Peaceful Coexistence. This will likely continue as growing economic incentives couple with existing military and diplomatic disincentives to give China a rational cost benefit to supporting regional stability and the maintenance of the status quo. Continued engagement, interdependence, and development will in turn foster the confidence and concomitant security which will better enable China to manage future crisis. Likewise, China's continuing focus on economic development will improve domestic stability, which is a precondition of political liberalization. However, history demonstrates that economic development cannot be achieved without military security. Evolutionary modernization in the PLA, lagging decades behind any notion of a modern force, must be accepted just as the West expects and demands improvements in its own military capabilities.

Within the scope of this case study, there exists no evidence of a deliberate policy of aggression or expansion, nor is there reason to anticipate such developments in the future, *provided* antagonisms based on misperception and self-fulfilling prophesies can be sufficiently controlled. This requirement obliges the West to analyze perspectives and legitimate interests objectively, as well as subjectively, from the perspective of China. The failure of China's military antagonists to do so in the past has contributed significantly to miscalculation and misperception, ultimately resulting in armed conflict.

SELECTED BIBLIOGRAPHY

Books

Acheson, Dean. *The Korean War.* New York: W. W. Norton Company, Inc., 1971.

Alexander, Bevin. *Korea, the First War We Lost.* New York: Hippocrene Books, 1986.

Bellows, Michael D., ed. *Asia in the 21st Century: Evolving Strategic Priorities.* Fort Lesley J. McNair, Washington, DC: National Defense University Press, Institute for National Strategic Studies, 1994.

Bercovitch, Jacob, and Richard Jackson. *International Conflict, A Chronological Encyclopedia of Conflicts and their Management, 1945-1995.* Washington DC: Congressional Quarterly, Inc., 1997.

Bernstein, Richard, and Ross H. Munro. *The Coming Conflict with China.* New York: Alfred A. Knopf, Inc., 1997.

Camilleri, Joseph. *Chinese Foreign Policy, the Maoist Era and its Aftermath.* Oxford: Martin Robertson, 1980.

Chakravarti, P. C. *India's China Policy.* Bloomington: Indiana University Press, 1962.

Chen, Jian. *China's Road to the Korean War: The Making of the Sino-American Confrontation.* New York. Columbia University Press, 1994.

Chen, King C. *China's War with Vietnam, 1979.* CA: Hoover Institution Press, 1987.

Clubb, Edmund O. *20th Century China*, 3d ed. New York: Columbia University Press, 1978.

Edwardes, Michael. *Nehru, a Political Biography.* New York: Praeger Publishers, 1971.

Foot, Rosemary. *The Wrong War.* Ithaca: Cornell University Press, 1985.

Gilks, Anne. *The Breakdown of the Sino-Vietnamese Alliance, 1970-1979.* Berkeley CA: University of California, Berkeley, Institute of East Asian Studies, Center for Chinese Studies, 1992.

Gill, Bates, and Lonnie Henley. *China and the Revolution in Military Affairs.* Carlisle Barracks, PA: Strategic Studies Institute, US Army War College, 1996.

Goncharov, Sergei N., John W. Lewis, and Xue Litai. *Uncertain Partners: Stalin, Mao, and the Korean War*. Stanford, CA: Stanford University Press, 1993.

Goulden, Joseph C. *The Untold Story of the Korean War*. New York: New York Times Books, 1982.

Hoyt, Edwin P. *The Day the Chinese Attacked*. New York: Paragon House, 1993.

Huntington, Samuel P. *The Clash of Civilizations, and the Remaking of the World Order*. New York: Touchtone Books, 1996.

Johnston, Alastair I. *Cultural Realism, Strategic Culture and Grand Strategy in Chinese History*. New Jersey: Princeton University Press, 1995.

Manchester, William. *American Caesar, Douglas MacArthur, 1880-1964*. Boston: Little, Brown, and Company, 1978.

Marshall, George C. *George C. Marshall, 1880-1959*. New York: George C. Marshall Foundation, 1987.

Maxwell, Neville. *India's China War*. New York: Anchor Books, 1972.

McGregor, Charles. *The Sino-Vietnamese Relationship and the Soviet Union*. London: USSA Adelphi Papers. Institute for International Strategic Studies, 1988.

Nathan, Andrew J., and Robert S. Ross. *The Great Wall and the Empty Fortress*. New York: W. W. Norton and Company, 1997.

Neustadt, Richard, and Ernest May. *Thinking in Time*. New York: Free Press, 1988.

O'Shaughnessy, John F. *The Chinese Intervention in Korea: an Analysis of Warning*. Master of Strategic Studies Thesis, Defense Intelligence Agency, Bowling AFB, 1985.

Palit, D. K. *War in the High Himalaya*. New York: Saint Martin's Press, 1991.

Pandey, B. N. *Nehru*. New York: Stein and Day, 1976.

Park, Mun Su. *The International Dimensions of the Korean War: Geopolitical Realism, Misperception, and Postrevisionism*. Ph.D. diss., University of New York, Buffalo, 1993.

Pillsbury, Michael. *Chinese Views of Future Warfare*. Washington, DC: National Defense University Press, 1997.

Smith, Dianne L., ed. *Asian Security to the Year 2000*. Carlisle Barracks, PA. Strategic Studies Institute, US Army War College, 1996.

Stoessinger, John G. *Why Nations go to War*, 3d ed. New York: St. Martin's Press, 1982.

Sun Tzu. *The Art of War*. Translated and with a forward by Samuel P.Griffith. New York: Oxford University Press, 1963.

Tien, Chen-ya. *Chinese Military Theory*. London: Mosaic Press, 1992.

Toffler, Alvin, and Heidi Toffler, *War and Anti-War, Survival in the 21st Century*. Boston: Little, Brown, and Company, 1993.

Truman, Harry S. *Memoirs by Harry S. Truman*. Vol. 2, *Years of Trial and Hope*. New York: Doubleday & Company, Inc., 1956.

Wang, James C. F. *Contemporary Chinese Politics*, 2d ed. Englewood Cliffs, NJ: University of Hawaii, Prentice-Hall, 1985.

Whiting, Allen S. *China Crosses the Yalu*. California: Stanford University Press, 1960.

Wilborn, Thomas L. *How Northeast Asians view their Security*. Carlisle Barracks, PA. Strategic Studies Institute, US Army War College, 1991.

Journals

Freeman, Chas W., "Preventing War in the Taiwan Strait." New York. Council on Foreign Relations, Inc., Foreign Affairs (July-August 1998): 7.

Grant, Richard L. "China and Southeast Asia." Vol. 15, no. 4, Center for Strategic and International Studies (July-August 1993): 3.

Hughes, Neil C. "Smashing the Rice Bowl." New York. Council on Foreign Relations, Inc., Foreign Affairs (July-August 1998): 67.

Lardy, Nicholas R. "China and the Asian Contagion." New York. Council on Foreign Relations, Inc., Foreign Affairs (July-August 1998): 78.

Yergn, Daniel. "Fueling Asia's Recovery." New York. Council on Foreign Relations, Inc., Foreign Affairs (March-April 1998): 35.

Internet

Bajanov, Evgueni. *Assessing the Politics of the Korean War, 1949-51*. Cold War International History Project Bulletin 6-7, Woodrow Wilson International Center for Scholars. Available from http://www.gwu.edu/nsarchive/cwihp.html. Internet. Accessed 30 January 1999.

Herschberg, James G. *New East-Block Documents on the Sino-Indian Conflict, 1959 & 1962*. Cold War International History Project Bulletin 8-9, Woodrow Wilson International Center for Scholars. Available from http://www.gwu.edu/nsarchive /cwihp.html. Internet. Accessed 30 January 1999.

Jian, Chen. *China's Road to the Korean War*. Cold War International History Project Bulletin 6-7, Woodrow Wilson International Center for Scholars. Avaialble from http://www. gwu.edu/nsarchive/cwihp.html. Internet. Accessed 30 January 1999.

Johnston, Alastair J. *Engaging Myths: Misconceptions about China and its Global Role*. Harvard Asia Pacific Review. Accessed from ttp:/www.hcs.harvard.edu/~haprW9 /98/johnston.html. Internet. Accessed 29 September 1998.

Rappai, M. V. *China's Military Modernization: Some Perspectives*. IDSA. Available from http://www.idsa-india.org/an-jan-2.html. Internet. Accessed 28 August 1998.

Mansourov, Alexandre Y. *Stalin, Mao, Kim, and China's Decision to Enter the Korean War, September 16-October 15, 1950: New Evidence from Russian Archives*. Cold War International History Project Bulletin 6-7, Woodrow Wilson International Center for Scholars. Available from http://www.gwu.edu/nsarchive/ cwihp.html. Internet. Accessed 30 January 1999.

National Center for Policy Analysis Idea House. *Will China be a Military Threat?* Available from http://www.ncpa.org/pi/congress/nat497a.html. Internet. Accessed 28 August 1998.

PERISCOPE, *China*. Available from http://www. periscope.ucg.com/nations/asia/china. Internet. Accessed 28 August 1998.

Prozumenshikov, M.Y. *The Sino-Indian Conflict, the Cuban Missile Crisis, and the Sino-Soviet Split, October, 1962: New Evidence from the Russian Archives*. Cold War International History Project Bulletin 8-9, Woodrow Wilson International Center for Scholars. Available from http://www. //www.gwu.edu/nsarchive/cwihp.html. Internet. Accessed 30 January 1999.

Smith, Richard J. "The Past in China's Present. An Historical Perspective on China's Contemporary Approach to International Relations." Rice University. Available from http://www.owlnet.rice.edu/~anth220/thepast.html. Internet. Accessed 9 October 1998.

Zhai, Qiang. *Beijing and the Vietnam Conflict, 1964-65: New Chinese Evidence, Article and Translations*. Cold War International History Project Bulletin 8-9, Woodrow Wilson International Center for Scholars. Available from http://www.gwu.edu/ nsarchive/ cwihp.html. Internet. Accessed 30 January 1999.

Other Media

Foreign Broadcast Information Service (FBIS). *Chinese White Paper on National Defense*. Beijing Xinhua: Information Office of the State Council of China,. 27 July 1998.

www.ingramcontent.com/pod-product-compliance
Lightning Source LLC
Chambersburg PA
CBHW081351280526
45788CB00009B/2840